The *Constance Spry*
Book of
Flower
Arranging

Harold Piercy

Sundial

First published in 1979 by
Sundial Books Limited
59 Grosvenor Street,
London W1

Illustrations: Hennerwood
Publications Limited
ISBN 0 904230 79 1

Printed in Great Britain by
Jarrold and Sons Limited

Contents

Introduction 8
Buying and growing flowers 10
The care of cut flowers 20
Containers 28
Mechanics 40
The principles of arrangement 48
Spring 56
Summer 68
Autumn 84
Winter 98
Flowers for children 112
Special arrangements 118
Dried flowers 130
A-Z reference 136
Index and acknowledgments 154

Introduction

There have been many books about arranging flowers and some have laid down rules and regulations to be followed, with emphasis on design, scale, balance, and harmony. No such rules are laboured here, because at the Flower School we encourage practical experience and personal taste. For instance, although much time and preparation should go into the selection of colours when arranging a group of flowers, the colour wheel should never be taken as the authority for colour combinations: flower arranging is an expression of your own sense of beauty. In this book I have tried just to be practical in my approach and pass on the tips which I have picked up over the years.

For instance, I found early on that it is wise to learn the correct names as you progress with flowers as these are universally understood. I was asked to use 'honesty' in a decoration and did so, only to discover that what I knew as honesty (*Lunaria biennis*) was not the same plant as her Ladyship wanted, and I should have used wild clematis (*Clematis vitalba*)!

I first met Constance Spry herself when once I gave a talk to an allotment association on growing flowers for cutting and she came to speak on flower arranging. At that time I knew her famous name and had one or two of her books, so I was thrilled when I found that she had been in the audience for part of my talk. She invited me to train at her Flower School and after the course I stayed to help the staff with the Coronation of Queen Elizabeth II. I must say straight away that I was only a junior and did more with a broom than with the flowers, but I was there!

The excitement of unpacking all the wonderful and unusual flowers sent from abroad was greater than any Christmas morning in my life. In those days air transport was very slow and packing flowers for transit of this kind was almost unknown. Much work had to be done to revive some of the flowers: we had coppers of water boiling so that, as they were unpacked, tired flowers were cut and their stems placed in warm water. There were hundreds of buckets in which to put the prepared blooms, which were placed on stands allotted to their country of origin, but I am quite certain that some countries accidentally got new varieties for the occasion!

When we had completed our work and everything was ready, Mrs. Spry gave us each a few leftover flowers to take home. Tears came to the eyes of my landlady as she hugged the 'Royal flowers', and all I had to arrange them in was a large pickle jar standing in a waste paper basket! I was too tired to worry, but I can still picture them in clashing red colours—a few strelitzia, roses, carnations, azaleas and some dark foliage—these were the materials left over from Westminster School Hall and a gift from the people of San Remo.

Immediately after this, the busiest week of my life, I was posted to look after the garden at Mrs. Spry's home in Berkshire. Mrs. Spry was so enthusiastic that it was a joy to work with her. She was always planning ahead and had a wonderful driving personality that kept you on your toes in the nicest way. Each year, we would be at the Chelsea Flower Show and even before it opened for the royal preview she would stand back and discuss the stand as a whole and details which she did not really think were quite right, saying, 'And next year, we must try   '

A few days after I started working with her she came into the potting shed early one morning and announced that I was to go to Bournemouth that very day to demonstrate to a flower club. She wouldn't listen to my protests so I had to go. All the way down on the train I worked out what I would talk about: care and handling, containers, wire netting, etc. How could I occupy the time and not have to arrange too many vases? I had done it all before in a very simple way, but never under the Spry flag.

Since then, however, I have given demonstrations in many countries such as Japan, India and South Africa. There are so many interesting new ideas and materials coming from other countries and we can learn much from them even though they may not all follow the same technique or styles of arrangement as we do; in Japan, for example, pinholders are used on their own without any trace of wire netting and are often a visible part of the arrangement. Only a few years ago when I was in Japan demonstrating, I had the greatest difficulty obtaining any wire netting at all, and this was disastrous at the time as I rely on netting as the very foundation for my arrangements.

Experience is the best teacher of flower arranging and during my years at Spry's I have been fortunate enough to visit royal palaces and many other wonderful homes with a team of decorators. In this book I have tried to pass on the experience I have gained through years of working with flowers, but there are no rules and Mrs' Spry's words still hold good; 'Never forget that in arranging flowers you have an opportunity to express your own sense of what is beautiful and you should feel free and uninhibited in doing so'.

LEFT This striking arrangement is the result of a careful selection of a variety of materials of interesting shape and colour. In the arrangement are *Escallonia, Clematis, Passiflora caerulea, Fuchsia, Geranium, Liriope*, and the foliage of *Astrantia, Euronymus*, and *Sedum*. The arrangement is done in a small block of Oasis, fitted in a polythene bag and placed in an alabaster urn.

PAGES 4–5 A simple arrangement of the side shoots or secondary shoots of single daisy type chrysanthemums with the addition of a few pompom dahlias. Foliages used are small pieces of *Aucuba japonica*, Golden privet and ivy trails. Flowers are placed in a small piece of Oasis standing in a carved wooden dish.

PAGES 6–7 An arrangement in the making: the various plant materials, which include *Pinus, Hedera, Hyacinthus*, and *Helleborus niger*, have all received the correct stem treatment to ensure that they will last well, and are positioned one by one in the container which has been prepared with wire netting and a pinholder.

Buying and growing flowers

Buying flowers

Naturally, flowers from a shop can be costly because of overheads but they should have received the proper treatment if the shop is a good one and this will certainly help them to last longer. Flowers keep best under cool airtight conditions, so those offered by a street trader may often have deteriorated after a day or so exposed to the cold or heat and perhaps a drying wind.

Always look at the foliage on cut flower stems and at the base of the stems, as discolouration indicates age and the smell will certainly give you an idea of the length of time that they have been standing in water.

Here are a few specific tips which may be helpful when buying flowers.

Iris, tulips, gladioli and daffodils should be bought when in bud, with the flower colour just showing. They will soon open in a warm place. Fresh daffodils once opened should make a rustling sound when shaken —those past their best will have soft petals which no longer make a sound and appear papery. Gladioli should have just the first flower open at the base of the spike. Some people recommend taking out the tip, which may help the other flowers to open right to the top.

Single daisy type flowers, for example all year round chrysanthemums (sometimes known as American spray chrysanthemums), should have a hard green centre with just a small ring of pollen showing yellow at the base of the petals: a raised centre disc of yellow (covered in pollen) means that flowering is nearly over.

Roses should always be bought as nicely shaped fat buds with good foliage right up the stem. Some varieties are much better than others at keeping their shape.

Mimosa should always be purchased from a polythene pack and never from outside in the open air: its pollen dries in the open air and sheds more quickly. Always look at it carefully to see that the small fluffy flowers which go together to make the compound spikes are just opening, and then it should last a little while.

Poppies should be showing only a trace of colour as the bud scales split because they open very quickly once in water.

As flowers are much more expensive than they used to be, many florists will sell individual flowers rather than bunches and so you can often buy the exact number that you need for an arrangement. Some florists will sell mixed bunches.

Many flowers are available for most of the year. Heaths and rhododendrons are a good example. Camellias start in January and go through to July, and hellebores go from November until July. Some glasshouse and outdoor crops have no specific season. Chrysanthemums are available all the year round, although they are much more prolific during certain months. Border carnations and anemones are available most of the year, and freesias are now joining them. Flowers will be cheapest in their natural season; if you require flowers out of their normal season, they will have been imported from abroad so there will be extra costs. Anything 'forced' to make it appear earlier than it would normally be available on the market will also be more expensive. With modern growing techniques, and rapid transport facilities, there is nothing that cannot be produced if you are prepared to pay the cost.

There is an unfortunate modern tendency for an increasing number of flowers to be dyed; I consider this to be a great pity, for there are so many beautiful flowers available in natural colours. Dyeing has been introduced by the commercial growers who produce one prolific crop of white flowers and colour them to suit demand. Some are extremely well done, but a dyed flower should never be used if a natural alternative is available.

The commercial market seldom caters for pretty foliages, and the flower arranger who has only a small garden, with little room to grow extra flowers for cutting, may find it helpful to grow some useful foliages to use with bought flowers for indoor arrangements.

PAGES 10–11 The Constance Spry flower shop in London.
BELOW Wild parsley and grasses placed in a beer mug make a simple decoration.

Wild flowers

Many wild flowers can be used very successfully in flower arrangements but there is now a law to protect wild plants from indiscriminate picking and virtually every species in this country (with the exception of a few poisonous weeds) has some measure of protection.

It is an offence for anyone to dig up a wild plant (including flowering plants, ferns, mosses, liverworts and lichens) without the permission of the owner or occupier of the land on which it grows.

Flowers and fruits can still be picked from wild plants but, since many countryside plants have become quite scarce, it is very important to pick with the greatest care, taking only from plants common in the locality and cutting very few pieces from each plant. If you find just a small group of something that attracts you, remove only one or two pieces and never take everything.

There are, however, twenty-one plants which are so rare that even picking would be harmful to them, and these plants, illustrated overleaf, are totally protected. Removal of any part of these plants is an offence under the *Conservation of Wild Creatures and Wild Plants Act 1975*. Copies of the Act may be obtained from HMSO bookshops.

When travelling in the countryside, it is useful to take a large polythene bag, a pair of scissors and a newspaper. If you cut anything, damp the newspaper and lay it carefully in the base of the polythene bag and then place the cut materials onto the paper as quickly and carefully as possible. Seal up the bag and keep it in a cool place until the materials can be sorted out and treated in the correct way. All flowers last best if kept cool and airtight.

ABOVE This arrangement in a small basket shows what can be done with a few flowers carefully picked from a country lane.

13

Protected wild plants

MEZEREON
Daphne mezereum

RED HELLEBORINE
Cephalanthera rubra

WILD GLADIOLUS
Gladiolus illyricus

OBLONG WOODSIA
Woodsia ilvensis

SPIKED SPEEDWELL
Veronica spicata

SNOWDON LILY
Lloydia serotina

ALPINE WOODSIA
Woodsia alpina

DIAPENSIA
Diapensia lapponica

DROOPING SAXIFRAGE
Saxifraga cernua

CHEDDAR PINK
Dianthus gratianopolitanus

ALPINE SOW-THISTLE
Cicerbita alpina

KILLARNEY FERN
Trichomanes speciosum

MILITARY ORCHID
Orchis militaris

MONKEY ORCHID
Orchis simia

LADY'S-SLIPPER
*Cypripedium
calceolus*

GHOST ORCHID
*Epipogium
aphyllum*

TEESDALE
SANDWORT
Minuartia stricta

TUFTED SAXIFRAGE
Saxifraga cespitosa

SPRING GENTIAN
Gentiana verna

BLUE HEATH
Phyllodoce caerulea

ALPINE GENTIAN
Gentiana nivalis

15

The flower arranger's garden

Half the fun of arranging flowers is in growing them for yourself. Mrs. Spry was a wonderful gardener and had a great knowledge of plants. If you are a good grower, you will usually find your tender care of the plants well rewarded by their longer life in your arrangement. Many students come to the Flower School after studying horticulture and it is quite noticeable how well they handle their materials as a result of knowing how much care has gone into producing the flowers and foliages. Similarly, many flower arrangers, having come to know and love the plants they use, develop an interest in growing their own materials.

Planning the garden

Personal taste plays a big part in what you grow; some people will go for a lot of colour, others may prefer shape and texture and be happy with only mixed green foliages. Whatever your preference, choose plants with your room colourings in mind and grow only the varieties or colours that will be of use to you when decorating.

If the garden is large enough it is a good idea to grow some plants solely for garden decoration and to have others in nursery rows for cutting purposes only, but in many cases there will not be enough room to grow all the materials required so very careful planning will be necessary.

If only a small space is available it may make sense to grow mostly foliage plants and shrubs and to buy the cut flowers from your local florist. Such a garden would also be labour-saving because once the plants are established they will need little attention. Evergreen shrubs, silver-grey foliages, and plants giving not only flowers but also Autumn colour and perhaps berries, are well worth considering for the small garden.

A walled garden is a great asset and can offer an extra source for cutting materials. For example, some of the old-fashioned climbing roses such as 'La Follette' would be suitable. The rose 'Constance Spry' flourishes as a free-growing rose in the border but with limited space it is worth trying against a wall. Clematis, passion flower, cobaea and ivies would also be excellent.

When planning the garden, remember to allow plants plenty of room to develop. Use mostly perennial plants and add interesting annuals, biennials and bulbs when space is available: this will allow the maximum amount of variety and the longest flowering period possible. A small heated greenhouse will greatly extend the growing season.

A little pruning may be necessary to keep the plants in good shape and the trimmings can be used in arrangements, but however much you may require certain pieces, be fair to the plant and do not over-prune as this will spoil its natural habit. The plant must have first priority! Always cut (never tug) to a growing point, and do not leave snags of wood to die back.

The positioning of each group of plants in the garden needs a great amount of care and the same rules should be observed here as for a flower arrangement. Try to keep different shaped foliages and colours next to each other, allowing for variation in height and bearing in mind the ultimate size to which the plant will grow. Poor planning and planting in the garden will worry the discerning eye just as much as incorrect placement of stems in a flower arrangement and, of course, it will be far more difficult to remedy without uprooting the plants.

RIGHT AND BELOW Interesting foliages are essential for flower arrangement and are well worth growing to supplement flowers bought from a florist. These pictures show the author's small city garden in Spring (right) with a planted trough in the foreground, and Autumn (below.)

16

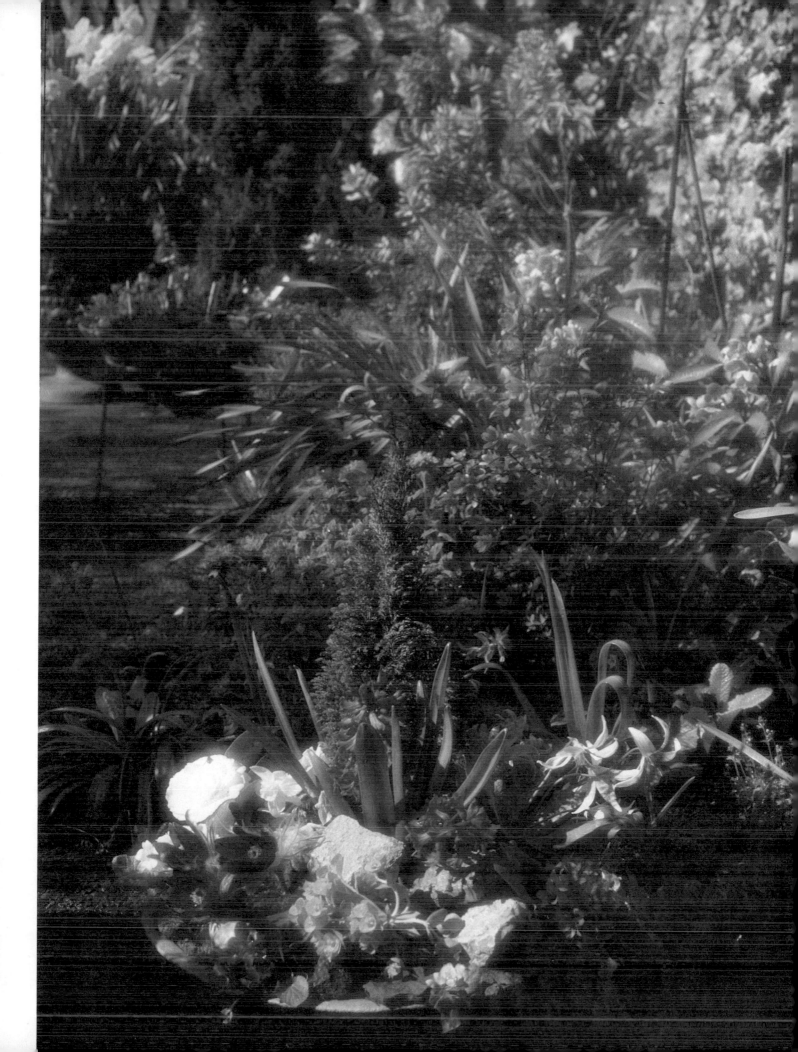

Cutting garden flowers

BELOW Another view of the author's small foliage garden in Autumn looking down on *Hebe, Azalea, Ruta, Laurus nobilis* and *Helleborus*, with a background of *Hedera*. See previous page.

When cutting flowers from the garden, carry a bucket of water with you and immediately each stem is cut, place it in the bucket. Do not leave it to dry out while gathering other flowers and never leave flowers in heaps on the ground to be collected at a later time. Wait until everything is gathered in the house or garden shed before grading it into stem categories for special treatment.

Always use a good pair of secateurs or scissors when cutting. Make a clean cut and never tug at the material or you may loosen the plant and cause it to die. Judicious pick-ing is a matter of great importance and no single plant should be cut too heavily, except annuals or biennials grown specifically for cutting. In fact, it is essential to keep cutting annuals if they are to flower over a long season. Once they have set seed, their life cycle is completed and they will stop flowering.

Much is said about not cutting flowers in the heat of the day. Commercial growers cut flowers at all hours until the crop is harvested, but I prefer to cut either in the early morning or the early evening, allowing the flowers to stand in a bucket of water and drink for a whole day or night before arranging them.

Senecio
Eucalyptus
Elaeagnus
Alnus
Bergenia
Alchemilla
Ruta
Hosta
Hedera

Foliages for the garden

Most of the materials listed below are not usually available from a florist and are well worth growing in the garden. Additional information is given at the end of this book about all these and other useful plants for the flower arranger, many of which can also be grown very successfully in the garden. Some plants, however, can be difficult to grow in certain soils without a lot of extra soil preparation and are quite costly to maintain over the years, so it is always wise to check with a reliable gardening authority before sowing or planting.

Acer
Alchemilla
Alnus glutinosa
Aralia elata
Arbutus unedo

Artemisia
Arum italicum
 pictum
Arundinaria
Aucuba japonica

Berberis
Bergenia
Betula
Bocconia cordata
Buxus
Camellia
Carpinus betulus
Cedrus
Cineraria maritima
Cornus mas
Corylopsis pauciflora
Corylus avellana
Cynara scolymus
Cytisus
Elaeagnus
Escallonia
Eucalyptus
Euonymus
Euphorbia
 epithymoides and
 E. wulfenii

Fagus
Foeniculum vulgare
Geranium
Hedera
Hosta
Ilex aquifolium
Lamium
Larix
Ligustrum
 ovalifolium 'Aureo
 Marginata'
Lonicera
Mahonia
Onopordon
Osmanthus
Paeonia
Phalaris
 arundinacea
Phormium tenax
Pieris
Polygonatum

Prunus
Pulmonaria
Pyracantha
Rhododendron
Ribes sanguineum
Rosmarinus
Ruta
Salix
Salvia
Santolina
Senecio laxifolius
Smilacina
Sorbus aria
 'Lutescens'
Spiraea
Stachys lanata
Symphoricarpos
Typha
Verbascum
Viburnum lantana
Vitis

The care of cut flowers

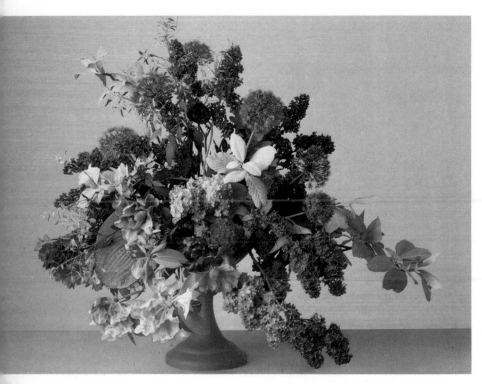

ABOVE This attractive arrangement in pink colourings includes a number of materials which require special stem treatment before arrangement. The woody stems of *Syringa*, *Sorbus aria lutescens*, and *Rhododendron* are hammered, and the *Tulipa* are wrapped in paper during their first drink. All leaves are removed from *Syringa* stems, and those of *Rhododendron* have been thinned to allow the flowers to show to good advantage. The main foliage in the arrangement comes from *Eucalyptus* and *Hosta*.

PAGES 20–1 A trug basket of flowers ready for stem treatment: soft stems are cut at an angle and woody stems are cut and hammered.

What is understood by the terms 'life of cut flowers' and 'lasting well'? A good example is the garden rose: if we pick it in bud and find that it gradually opens up in water, until it is full blown and the petals begin to fall from the stem, we know that we have seen it at its best. Even on the bush in the garden it would probably not have had a longer life. Conversely, if the rose droops while still in bud and gradually shrivels, this indicates that we have not treated it properly and that it has suffered a premature death.

The lasting qualities of flowers and foliages once cut vary considerably, but a lot can be done to extend their life by a few days, and it is well worth all the effort. It is very sad to think of the time and care that goes into producing a crop of flowers being wasted because of a little lack of attention to the cut stems.

The correct stage at which the flowers are cut is very important and the time between cutting and placing in water plays a large part in keeping certain flowers alive. Flowers picked when fully open cannot be expected to last as long as buds which are just opening. On the other hand, if a flower is picked too early, it will never develop into its true full-sized bloom.

A collection of containers ranging from a deep bucket to a shallow dish will be needed. Some flowers should have a long drink in fairly shallow water (daffodils and narcissi, for example), others such as anemones and hellebores require saturating in deep water before being used. All containers should be thoroughly cleaned before being used. Fresh water from the tap is best for all flowers and the temperature may be varied according to the specific needs of the plant material. Water collected in water butts or from a pond in the garden should not be used as it is teeming with bacteria which will readily breed in the warm conditions inside the house. Bacteria make the water smell unpleasant and block the stem vascular tissue which will result in poor water absorption and so greatly reduce the life of the flowers. The addition of chemicals to the water extends the life of some flowers and is worth considering, especially for showing. Chrysal, a popular proprietary substance which has been introduced from Holland, is a plant food which contains a stimulant and disinfectant. It should be used strictly according to instructions. It will make materials last a few days longer and flowers grow and develop well when arranged in it.

The main points for the care of cut flowers and foliage are:

Put materials into water as soon as possible after cutting.

⚓ Always use clean water.

⚓ Stand materials in a cool place to have a long drink, preferably overnight, before arranging.

⚓ Anything which has wilted should go into really warm water.

⚓ Spray overhead with a fine mist of water to charge the air with moisture.

⚓ No foliage should remain on any stem which when arranged will be below the water line.

⚓ All flowers should have their stems cut at an angle so that if they should slip to the bottom of a dirty container the stem cannot fall flat on the base and perhaps stop the intake of moisture.

⚓ Remove any broken stems or leaves, and thin out unwanted shoots.

Flowers and foliages can be brought forward a little after cutting by being placed in warm water in a warm place, adding more warm water as necessary. Keep the atmosphere around them very moist by spraying continually with a fine mist of water to create a feeling of April showers and soften the bud scales, enabling them to open more readily. Never attempt to open flowers with your fingers or mechanical aids; you will bruise the delicate, immature flower petals and as they open they will be badly marked.

Most cut flowers cannot stand hot dry air for long. It soon robs them of their natural moisture and causes them to wilt and die. They should be protected from the direct rays of hot sunshine. In heated rooms the most that can be done is to see that the flowers are not subjected to direct heat. Place them as far away as possible from heat sources and pay special attention to keeping

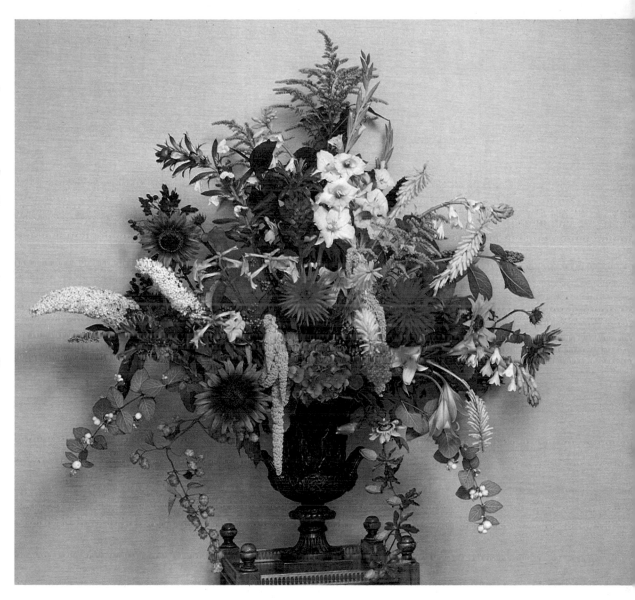

the vases topped up with water.

Draughts can kill flowers, too, especially those which have been brought in from the moist warm air of the glasshouse.

Certain flowers drink a surprising amount of water during the first few hours after arrangement. The vase should be filled up to the brim when the arrangement is finished and should be topped up with warm water within a few hours if necessary. There is no need to change the water in an arrangement if all leaves have been kept away from the water level and if clean stems and a clean vase were used.

Whether they have been bought from a flower shop or picked from the garden, all flowers and foliages should be properly treated before being arranged in a vase. There are particular treatments for each stem group and different soils and methods of cultivation also have a bearing on the way in which garden flowers should be treated. Flowers that do not respond to one

treatment may well benefit from another, and the best method is found by trial and error. Only by constant observation and experiment do we become aware of how flowers respond to the different treatments.

The great interest in flower arrangement shown by so many people today has resulted in many useful discoveries and recommendations for making flowers last, although often these have no scientific background. It is certainly no old wives' tale that flowers last well in metal containers and that aspirin helps to keep flowers fresh; the aspirin slows down the breeding rate of the bacteria and so helps the plant material to take up water. A copper penny in the water gives off a trace of copper which acts on the bacteria in the same way. A few drops of weak disinfectant in the water will also keep it sweet-smelling. Never dismiss a suggestion without first trying it; it may well help, and all the suggested treatments have resulted from experiments in the first instance.

Hard woody stems

Many useful flowers and foliages fit into this group. All the main trees, shrubs and blossoms—apple, cherry and plum, for example—come into this class, together with stocks, outdoor chrysanthemum and wall-flowers. These stems should be cut at an angle and, if they are very woody, an inch of bark should be removed from their base so that the cambium layer (the white stem beneath the bark) shows clearly. The stem is then split with a strong pair of secateurs, or hammered to break up the fibres. Any foliage that would appear below the water level should be cut off and any damaged or un-wanted shoots trimmed out before the stem is placed in a bucket of deep water. If there has been a time lag between cutting the branches of foliage and getting them into water, it is a good idea to place the tips in really hot water for a few minutes immediately before standing them in warm water for a long drink.

Lilac comes in two very different forms. The forced Dutch lilac, which is with us during December to the end of March, has very long straight stems with little or no foliage and a large flower head at the top. The main colour is white, but a little mauve is often available. These stems should be hammered and placed in very hot water for a long drink. If the flowers wilt they should be sprayed with a fine mist of cold water, and

their stems should be re-cut, put in hot water and left to stand in a cool place for a few hours. If bought in good condition, forced lilac can last up to ten days. It is an ideal flower to have for a large group in early Spring.

Garden lilac in its many colours, picked during May and June, is full of leaf and this presents a problem. The stems are not usually straight and often carry a number of flower heads and many clusters of leaves. The stems cannot support this burden and the flower heads at the tips of the stems wilt due to insufficient water reaching them. The solution is to remove all the leaves and short foliage shoots from the flowering stems, and arrange the shoots separately among the flowering stems in the vase. The woody stems are treated in exactly the same way as the forced lilac.

Soft stems

This group of materials have soft succulent stems; examples are arum lilies and clivia. Their stems should be cut at an angle and placed straight away in deep water. Hyacinths and narcissi, which also come into this class, both exude a slimy sap which can damage other flowers. They should be cut and placed in water on their own until the sap has seeped from the cut stem, a matter of an hour or so, and then put into fresh clean water, when they will be ready to arrange as you choose.

Tulips should have their soft stems cut cleanly at an angle and if they are rather thick split them for 1 cm (½ inch). Remove the bottom leaves and place all the heads level, rolling bunches of ten or so stems together in stiff 'wet-wrapping' paper (a type of greaseproof paper), just covering the flower heads to keep them in an upright position. This will stop the flower heads from falling forward and breaking off. Place them in a deep container of tepid water for a long drink before removing the paper. Some people suggest feeding tulips with a sugar solution but I find this unnecessary. Once arranged they should take up graceful curves and continue to grow. Arrange tulips one or two days before they are wanted to give them time to take up their curves.

Lily-of-the-valley is available in a forced form during most of the year but because it is very costly to produce, I seldom use it except for special occasions. It is sold attached to its pencil-thick roots which are wrapped in newspaper, and these should be cut off straight away. The tips of the cut stems are then lightly crushed and placed in warm water in a cool place for a few hours. Forced lily-of-the-valley has very pale green foliage, long fragile stems with bells more widely spaced than those from the garden, and a very delicate scent. It has quite good lasting qualities. The lily-of-the-valley from the garden is available from May to July, depending on which part of the country it grows in. It has shorter, more woody stems

with many more bells, dark green foliage and a much stronger scent. Unfortunately it does not last long, but to prolong its life as much as possible crush the stems and place them in warm water.

Hollow-stemmed flowers

Examples of these are large delphiniums, lupins, hollyhock and large dahlias. Their life will be extended a little if immediately after cutting they are inverted and their hollow stems filled with warm water from a small can and plugged with cotton wool before being returned to the bucket.

Amaryllis comes into this group, but needs even more care. The flower head is often so heavy that it will snap off just at the neck of the stem. A piece of split bamboo cane placed in the centre of the stem will give it the necessary support, but be careful not to puncture the stem with the cane. Fill the supported stem with water and plug it with cotton wool. It may also be helpful to place an elastic band around the base of the stem to stop it splitting and curling up.

Stems which bleed

Euphorbias and poppies belong to this group. Dandelions are an example of stems which bleed; when they are picked a white ring of thick, milky sap forms at the cut surface. You can either singe the cut tip of the stem in a candle flame for a few seconds or place

BELOW Stem treatments. From left to right: a stem of *Helleborus foetidus* which has started to go to seed. At this stage of development these stems take water well and just require a clean slanting cut. *Amaryllis* stems should be supported with a thin stick, then filled with water and plugged with cotton wool. *Euphorbia palustris* is a stem which bleeds and the cut stem tip must be sealed with a flame or boiling water before being placed in warm water.

the tips in shallow boiling water for thirty seconds, taking care to protect the rest of the stem from the steam. The poinsettia, which is a euphorbia, poses an extra problem; if any leaf is removed during arranging, the scar should be sealed by a candle flame.

Hellebores are really valuable flowers for the arranger. Flower colours are from pure white to pinks, mauves and dark purple and a fine range of pale greens. *Helleborus foetidus* is a very useful hellebore and can be cut from February to the end of June. The other forms start in November and go through to May.

Hellebores last well while growing in the garden but as they like moisture and coolness it takes a time to acclimatize them to room temperatures. Always place hellebores in warm water immediately after cutting. The stem length will vary considerably with season and variety but should never be allowed to dry out. Some people recommend putting pin pricks right up the stem to the flower head; others make a razor cut straight up the stem; and some arrangers make a small hole right through the stem just below the flower head. These treatments help young flowers to take up water, but once the seed pods have formed and the stem tissue has matured, no such treatment will be necessary. All hellebores should have the extreme tips of their stems placed in boiling water for thirty seconds, with the heads

protected from the steam. Then give them a long drink in deep warm water, allowing it to cool naturally, and cut away the damaged stem tip before arranging. It is always important to arrange these flowers with their stems fully immersed in water, and when they show signs of wilting to treat them as before with hot water. Unfortunately, the more beautiful the flower, the more quickly it is likely to go down.

Roses call for special treatment, particularly the long-stemmed ones from the florist. The length of the stem controls the price of the rose, so it is hard to understand why long-stemmed roses are so popular, as most roses do not last well if left at their full length. Also, the stems are often so long that the arranger has no container in which to place them and is forced to cut them shorter!

Unless one is to be used as a specimen in a single rose container, roses should have all their thorns removed, either by rubbing (running the back of a closed pair of scissors along the stem) or by cutting them from the stem. Any excess foliage should also be removed straight away. Garden roses seldom wilt when cut and may be placed in deep water immediately after cutting. If they are at all limp, glasshouse roses should be wrapped in a roll of stiff paper and given a long drink prior to arranging. As the flower head is at the point farthest away from the

BELOW Stem treatments. From left to right: *Hydrangea* flowers will only last as cut flowers if borne on one- or two-year old wood. The darker colour of the second-year wood shows up clearly here.
Rosa should be dethorned and have unnecessary foliage removed.

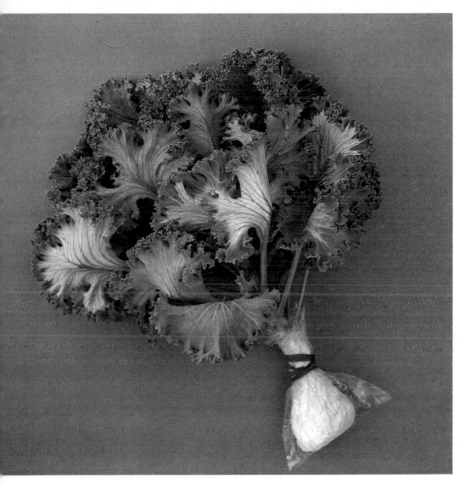

ABOVE Decorative cabbage. Wrap smelly stems such as this in cotton wool treated with disinfectant and place them in a polythene bag before putting them in an arrangement.

water, it is the first to wilt, and if this happens it may crack the stem tissue making it impossible to straighten the stem and revive the flower. At the first sign of wilting, the wrapping treatment must be carried out again. Recut the stems and split them, place the tips in boiling water for thirty seconds, then wrap the stems and flowers in stiff paper and give them a long drink in lukewarm water. Alternatively, recut the stems and submerge the whole flower and stem in a bath of water for a couple of hours, then place them in deep water in a cool place.

Some roses are much longer lasting than others. The old-fashioned roses, such as 'Madame Pierre Oger' and 'Cardinal de Richelieu', which are so much in demand these days, tend to be short lived but carry so many buds that when one flower goes over, another often manages to take its place, thus extending its decorative life.

Smelly stems

Flowers or foliages which are known to smell when arranged in water, such as a large stem of decorative cabbage, are best used with the cut stem isolated from the water in the vase. Wrap the stem in a pad of wet cotton wool treated with a disinfectant and place it in a small polythene bag.

Special treatments

Mimosa How often does one hear people say 'I don't use mimosa because it doesn't last'? Unfortunately, this is very true when it is arranged in a warm dry room. Mimosa is only fluffy when the flowers are fully out and covered with pollen, towards the end of the life of the flower. Once the pollen is shed, fertilization takes place, and the flower dies at the expense of a developing seed capsule.

It is necessary to retard the development of the pollen and this can be done by keeping the stems of mimosa in a polythene bag in a damp cool place. Once arranged, it should be kept as cool as possible. It is best to make one large arrangement of it for a special occasion (never mix it with other flowers) and enjoy it for the short time you have it. If using it for a party decoration, always leave its arrangement until just before it is required to see it at its best. Never use mimosa in table decorations because its smell will taint food very quickly.

Violets Unfortunately, the day of the lovely scented violet has nearly passed, and we no longer receive those that used to come from the south of France. The short Herrick violet, very dark in colour and scentless, is our main variety nowadays but even this is less common.

Violets absorb water through their heads so it is important always to keep moisture around them. Always arrange them in little clumps and keep the heads wet by immersing them in water for a short period each day. They look best in little moss gardens or tucked down deep among other Spring flowers as a table centrepiece.

Hydrangea This is usually used as a pot plant in the early part of the Summer and cut from the bush in the latter part of the year. It is important to see that the flower head is borne on one- or two-year-old wood (stems of pencil thickness) because the older, thicker branches will not take up water properly. Hydrangeas can be placed under water for a few hours to be really charged with moisture before use in an arrangement. If the flower has been forced it tends to be very soft and it will not stand up as a cut flower in a warm room, so it is better to remove some of the soil from a pot plant, pack the ball of roots in damp moss in a polythene bag, and place this in the centre of the flower group to get the effect of cut stems. In the latter part of the year, hydrangeas will dry naturally in a vase.

Sweet peas The petals go papery if allowed to remain wet so only spray them very lightly overhead. Cut the stems at an angle and place them in deep water for a long drink before arranging them.

Containers

ABOVE A clear glass basket holds the delicate stems of *Convallaria majalis* with its own foliage and a few of the first flowers of the small climbing rose 'Cecile Brunner'. Note how the roses have been brought through the arrangement, keeping the open (heavier) flowers in the centre.

PAGES 28–9 A variety of containers, including some which were not specifically designed for flowers but can be useful such as the sea shell, fruit dish and glass goblet.

The main purpose of arranging flowers is to see that they are presented in the most satisfactory and effective way possible. Great care must be given to shape, proportion and colour and there must be compatibility between the vase and flowers. The shape and height of the vase plays an important part in achieving the correct final result; top-heavy arrangements, groups that are too squat or skimpy, delicate flowers in too overpowering a vase or heavy flowers in a delicate one, will all offend the discerning eye.

On occasions the vase may be almost as important as the flowers themselves, particularly when you have just a few flowers to be arranged elegantly. There are times, however, when the vase serves solely as a container for water in which the flowers are anchored—even a baking tin can take an arrangement if it is concealed by the flowers or foliage.

To a certain extent, fashion dictates the use of some vases. The épergne and silver trumpet vase have had their turn and are seldom seen today, but that does not mean they will not come back. Many of us wish that the vases of our grandparents' day had been saved for our use; they would often solve the problem of the right vase for the occasion!

Glass

Many modern glass vases are designed to be ornaments and in no way are they really safe to use for flower arrangements. I look with horror at some of the designs I see on sale. If you are choosing glass, aim at a shape such as a basket, short-stemmed chalice or tazza which has a firm and heavy base and room to hide the netting under the flowers so that a confusion of stems and netting does not spoil the finished picture.

Glass must be kept perfectly clean and polished and always washed with soap and water immediately after use. A watermark easily occurs and this must be removed regularly otherwise it will become permanent. A piece of lemon dipped in salt and rubbed round the rim will help to remove stains. Bleach and disinfectants are also useful. As a last resort you can use a little hydrochloric acid for really badly marked glass, although this must be done with great care under the chemist's instruction and rubber gloves must be worn.

Probably the least useful glass vase is the cut glass vase or fruit bowl. The true beauty of cut glass is only seen when the light passes through it and produces excellent colour reflections; when filled with flowers the reflections are lost. Many of the vase shapes found in cut glass could easily be replaced with ordinary pottery vases, which would hold the flowers in exactly the same way without creating the problem of hiding the wire netting and flower stems.

Old-fashioned milk glass or a really beautiful clear goblet both look enchanting for well arranged flowers, and for the centre-piece of a modern table setting, one of the brandy-type glasses from the Scandinavian countries could look superb holding a floating open rose. A modern shallow glass on a long stem looks excellent for a small party with a candle in the centre and the flowers high above the table to be well away from the food. One flower ideally suited to a balloon glass is the violet: a bunch of violets, lightly tied, resting in the centre of the glass base makes a very pretty setting and they will last much longer in the moist atmosphere of the glass interior.

The glass specimen vase excellently displays the beauty of a single rose. Unfortunately many of these vases are so badly designed that they easily topple over when, for example, the rose opens its petals. Choose a sensible design which has a firm solid base and is not too tall. The rose stem in a specimen vase should retain its thorns because these produce the bubbles which are attractive magnified by the glass.

Marble and alabaster

Marble has the advantage of being very heavy, so over-balancing will not be a problem. Alabaster is not so heavy and is far more fragile. Both are sought after by flower arrangers and are now fairly rare to find and very expensive. The bigger vases are often put together with glue and care must be taken not to get the joints wet because they could soften and fall apart. Always provide waterproof linings for such vases. Remember, too, that water roughens the surface of alabaster vases after a time and heat causes it to lose its translucence and makes it opaque, so do not let a good tazza stand in the window in full sun for week on end. Wipe over alabaster vases with a good quality olive oil from time to time as this will help to keep them in good condition.

Imitation marble and soapstone
There are a few very good cherub-type vases and chalices made from a composition which really does resemble the valuable marble and soapstone carved vases; it is heavier than plastic and the vases are normally quite well balanced. Careful selection and choice of colour will reward you with a very useful vase which may be suitable for a wide range of materials.

ABOVE Five 'Golden Rain' roses at different stages of their development arranged in a heavy crystal pot.
ABOVE LEFT a good design of specimen vase holding two 'Paul's Scarlet' rose stems.

China vases

Simplicity of shape is important for all containers and a plain colour is much easier to use than one which is gaily ornamented or highly coloured as these will restrict the materials which may be used.

Some coloured vases can only be used for certain flowers: I have in mind a glorious little black vase of mine with beautiful china auricula flowers modelled on its sides. It is just right when auriculas can be used to fill it but when their short season of flowering is over other flowers look quite wrong in it.

Antique white china vases, with a painting of a mixed bunch of flowers, are lovely filled with simple mixed flowers which pick up the colours on the vase. If the vase has a scalloped edge care must be taken when moving it, otherwise it will readily allow a flow of water down the side! There are modern equivalents but they are often a poor shape and badly painted and look unsightly when filled with flowers.

If one has room for only a few vases, keep to the simple shapes and plain coloured ones —black, white, celadon green, grey and pewter colourings are the safest, as bright colours can be difficult to use.

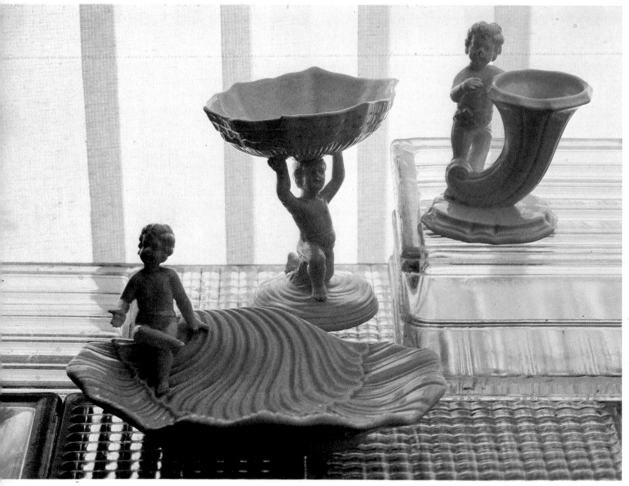

ABOVE This dolphin vase holds a small block of Oasis in which some interesting flowers are placed. The tall flowers at the back are *Lilium martagon album*, *Hoya carnosa* are the large, almost artificial-looking pink flowers in front, and sprays of wild strawberries flow over on the right. Other foliages in the arrangement are Variegated ivy and ivy-leafed *Geranium* 'Sussex Lace'.
LEFT Three amusing cupid-type vases.

32

Cupids

The cupid-type vases are very popular and over the last ten years have appeared in many shapes and sizes. The Victorian ones, which can be expensive, are fine figures but some modern ones can also be very good. Cupid vases can take all types of flowers but they must be in proportion to the size of the vase. Cherubs labouring under great weights spoil the whole picture. I often smile when I hear a prospective purchaser in the flower shop saying, 'Have you got a good-looking boy?', but they are quite right; some seem quite cherubic from a distance but on close inspection the little faces look quite dis-gruntled! Perhaps they are worried about the weight they may have to carry!

Many cupid vases have scalloped edges, and care must be taken when filling and moving these vases as it is easy to spill the water. Cupid dishes sold as soap dishes can also make interesting containers, see for example the arrangement on page 89.

ABOVE An ornate fan-shaped vase with a scalloped edge, with an arrangement of Spring flowers – *Osmanthus, Freesia, Fritillaria, Ranunculus, Helleborus foetidus, Myosotis, Scilla nutans, Muscari, Rosa, Narcissus, Hyacinthus, Eucalyptus, Allium, Pulsatilla.*

Baskets

There is a very large range of baskets which can be used for flowers today. They are usually made from rattan and cane and are imported from such places as the Far East, Portugal and Spain and come in many different shapes. Some baskets are made in England, but they are usually made in willow, which is more substantial than rattan and cane and appears heavier.

Most baskets have no lining so a container has to be found in which the flowers can be placed so as to appear as if they are arranged in the basket. Some people put the stems straight into one of the water-retaining foams wrapped in polythene to keep it moist and stop water dripping out. A glass pie dish is ideal for an oblong basket, and there are many bowls which will fit in a round basket.

Some baskets have metal linings and these are usually satisfactory but need painting to prevent them rusting; others may have a thin moulded plastic lining which eliminates rust but can be punctured easily when the netting is being fixed. Once the netting is fitted to the container it is best to leave it there and not to keep taking it in and out. This will also prevent the galvanizing on the netting from becoming cracked.

The large gilt Gainsborough basket, that tall high-handled shape that used to be so popular, is seldom seen today: it is expensive to buy and requires a lot of flowers to fill it. Another basket with a fairly high handle going from side to side, the big gilt oval-faced basket, is more likely to be seen filled with fruit at the back of a buffet table than filled with flowers but it is sometimes used for special occasions.

Baskets lend themselves to simple arrangements and look better in a cottage-type sitting room than in the grandeur of a large drawing room. Tiny square, oblong and round baskets are beautiful when arranged simply with mixed Spring or Summer flowers. They can also be filled with just one kind of flower.

LEFT ABOVE A collection of late-Summer garden flowers arranged in a Sussex trug. The flowers and foliages have been grouped together to avoid the spotty effect which often occurs in mixed groups.
LEFT BELOW An oval cane hamper basket with its lid propped open, filled with Michaelmas daisies.
BELOW Basket-type containers come in a variety of shapes, sizes and materials.

Wooden containers

Wood can be a sympathetic material for a container but it must have a waterproof lining.

The wooden trug—a speciality of the Sussex craftsman—is really a basket-type container (see page 34). A pie-dish is an ideal lining and can be bedded on moss or tissue paper to get it to fit firmly and level in the boat-shaped base of the basket. It looks particularly attractive filled with the more solid types of flowers, such as marigolds, wallflowers and sunflowers or, again, mixed collections of garden flowers.

Wooden boxes, such as those made in mahogany, make beautiful containers for flowers and are ideally suited to stand on a dresser or sideboard. Any interior fixtures will have to be taken out and a tin of suitable size (again, a baking tin is often ideal) used for a lining; sometimes the lid may be lined with velvet and this can be a feature; do not destroy it because the lid must be set up when the box is in use.

Wooden bowls, small half barrels, tubs and old wooden cheese presses make good cut-flower containers but are more likely to be filled with growing plants. This is perhaps due to the amount of cut flowers that are needed to fill them, and longer lasting plants would be cheaper to use in the long run.

Metal containers

Pewter

This is a useful colour for flowers, especially greys, mauves, purples and pinks. Many old pewter jugs, measures and mugs have pleasing lines and are easy to arrange. Flowers certainly last well in this type of container. A pewter plate is also a useful addition to a flower arranger's props—it will look good as a background and also be fun for a small arrangement. A pewter plate could also be used for a miniature garden, see page 116.

Silver

Silver is not often used nowadays compared with Victorian times, when trumpet vases and rose bowls were in most vase cupboards. A small silver basket or rose bowl remains perfect for a table setting but take care to line the vase first with brown paper, plastic or foil before placing wire netting into the container, and always clean the silver thoroughly after use. Silver demands certain types of flowers, as it can be so bright and shiny that it competes with the flowers. It takes soft delicate colours (mauves and pinks) and something rather sophisticated; on the other hand, some wild flowers, such as bluebells arranged with lacy foliage, can look very beautiful arranged in a silver sauce boat, for example.

RIGHT A variety of metal containers including a pewter jug, a silver rose bowl, a copper trough, a brass bowl with fluted edges and a copper jelly mould.
RIGHT BELOW *Gentiana sino-ornata* with *Graphaleum* flower buds and *Cineraria* leaves arranged on a pewter plate with lumps of crystal which look like ice.
BELOW The brightness of a silver container can make the flowers appear dull and must be used with care. Here an octagonal vase takes a mixed pink arrangement of *Astrantia, Alchemilla, Alstroemeria, Helleborus, Dianthus barbatus,* and *Sisyrinchium.*

Copper and brass

There are many good containers in these metals that were not designed to hold flowers yet are ideal for them, including such old kitchen equipment as saucepans, fish kettles and jelly moulds. The problem is to keep the containers clean and free from water marks which are difficult to clean off. Bad stains can be removed with salt and lemon or salt and vinegar: rub the surface really hard with a coarse cloth, rinse off and dry it thoroughly. Lacquering may be acceptable to some people to protect the metal but it detracts from the natural warm look, and the patina acquired over the years of cleaning with a soft cloth is lost. Once the lacquer starts to wear off, it will also be very difficult to get the container clean again.

Old copper has a pinkish tint to it and is much warmer-looking than brass; it lends itself to many of the soft apricot shades and Autumn tints. Brass is cooler and very attractive when used in conjunction with creams and lime greens. Both metals are excellent and the keen flower arranger is wise to collect as many shapes as possible.

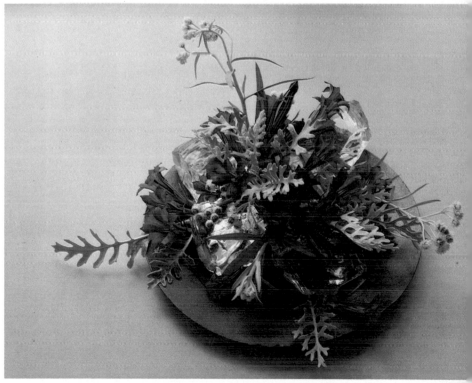

Bronze

Few people have bronze vases today, but one very elegant shape is the 'Warwick cup' which is well-balanced and heavy.

A bronze vase calls for heavy looking flowers—you must, in fact, let the weight and importance of your flowers be reflected in the vase. You may safely fill it with heavy materials in proportion to its size.

Lead

At one time lead was favoured in the making of urns and window boxes for outside decoration but only a few of these remain. Lead is heavy but soft and tends to split if not handled with care.

Wall vases

These can show flowers to really good advantage but great care must be taken to see that no syphoning of water occurs: the water level must be kept 1 cm (½ inch) below the rim of the vase and no leaf should hang over the rim at back or sides, otherwise the wallpaper may be marked. Fix the vase at the correct height and arrange the flowers with good downflowing lines.

LEFT The three-legged stand holding a glass dish, designed by Constance Spry for the Coronation. An arrangement of *Iris* leaves, *Delphinium*, *Clematis vitalba*, *Dianthus*, *Hydrangea*, *Scabious*, *Zinnia* 'Envy', *Nicotiana*, *Amaranthus caudatus* 'Viridis', *Aruncus*, *Eucalyptus*.

RIGHT The mirror trough, designed by Constance Spry. In the arrangement are *Erythronium*, *Hyacinthus orientalis*, *Phalaris arundinacea variegata*, *Helleborus orientalis*, *Hedera*, *Narcissus triandrus*, *Hebe*, *Polygonatum*.

LEFT Wall vases can be very useful, especially at parties. The flowers can be seen by everyone, yet kept well out of the way. In this arrangement are *Chaenomeles, Solidago, Hosta, Amaranthus caudatus* 'Viridis', *Helianthus, Nicotiana, Alchemilla, Chrysanthemum, Phalaris.*

Plastic and fibreglass

Although many people hate plastic, especially with flowers, little posy dishes and a few vases are quite useful and fairly cheap. The lightness of plastic may be a problem with some of the upright cherub type vases if they are not properly balanced. It may prove helpful to drill a hole in the back of the vase, fairly high up, and fill it with fine sand.

If you use plastic containers, keep to the white, black or green/white matt finishes, and look for a simple, pleasing shape. Very bright and shiny colours are rarely attractive for flowers in everyday use, although there are instances where brightly coloured plastic could be suitable. For example, the table for a children's party would look very gay with red, orange or yellow beakers and a centrepiece of Iceland or Californian poppies, arranged in a matching beaker or bowl, all on a brown hessian tablecloth.

Fibreglass is very strong yet light to handle and makes very good vases, especially the lead imitation which really does look natural. Again, being light, such a vase may fall over when full of tall foliage, etc., and it is a good idea to fill the base of the moulding with sand or gravel. Fibreglass pedestals are also useful and they can be painted any colour to suit the décor and should be filled with sand for safety.

Improvised vases

For the Coronation Mrs. Spry used two clever ideas; they were simple but adequate, and not too costly because we were still getting over the aftermath of World War II.

The first vase had to be suitable to stand on a round table seating about ten people. It was constructed of thin twisted wrought iron which was made into a three-legged stand and in this rested a glass dish. For a special effect the wrought iron was lightly touched with gold and a gold crown was fixed around the glass dish. The crown was made from buckram coated with gold paint, and on it were glued costume jewellery and a band of red velvet and mock ermine (white cellulose wool with black spots painted on it). These vases held the red flowers (including roses, carnations, azaleas) which were sent from San Remo. The vases stood on a tablecloth of pale blue silk and around the base of each vase was a garland of gold leaves and roses, made of artificial material. The cloth was finished with the E II R motif at four points.

The other vase, used for much larger arrangements on the buffet tables around the room, was designed on the same principle but, instead of glass dishes, large antique silver meat dish covers were used. The covers were turned upside down and were held in wrought iron stands.

Mechanics

PAGES 40–1 A
selection of
mechanics used in
flower arranging,
including a
pinholder, wire
netting, pebbles,
plastic foam.
BELOW Methods of
securing the netting:
tying it like a parcel
(left) and clipping
the ends of the wire
into the basketwork
(right). An end of
netting fixed round
an awkward stem
provides useful
support.

The mechanics are the means by which
flowers can be positioned exactly as required
within the container. They are essential to
flower arranging as they are the foundation
of the whole structure. So often one hears
people say, 'I know what I want, but I can
never get the flowers to stay in the correct
place'. Once you understand the mechanics,
however, you will find that you can work
easily and with real pleasure.

Flower arranging has progressed a good
deal since the days when flowers were stood
in vases which had been stuffed with stems
of evergreen to make the flowers all stand
up straight, although this method is still
used by some growers when showing their
best garden blooms at the local flower show.

The mechanics should allow everything
in the arrangement to have room and show
to good advantage, the stems flowing gracefully from the centre of the vase and not
standing at awkward angles, but the mechanics themselves must never show, whether
they are wire netting, Oasis or any other aid.

Wire netting

Ordinary wire netting is the most generally
useful of all the flower supporters. It should
be fairly pliable and of a large mesh, 5 cm
(2 inch) 0·71 mm (22 gauge) is the best because
this will hold firmly yet bends easily in the
hand. Never use the small-mesh netting
because it is too rigid and when folded up
will allow only the very thinnest stem entry
into the vase.

Keep the netting clean and dry when not
in use and it will last a long time. Always
keep the same piece for each vase so you will
not need to keep bending it to change the
shape. Folding and bending cracks the galvanizing, causing the wire to rust and
deteriorate rapidly. The amount of netting
needed will depend on the shape and size of
the vase but one should always aim to get
four or five layers of netting in an upright
vase, with the first layer just resting on the
bottom. In a shallow dish three to four layers
will be enough, especially in combination

42

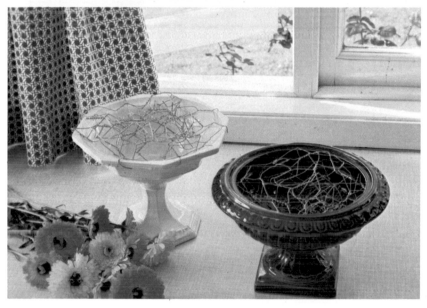

ABOVE Securing the netting on vases with outcurving (left) and incurving (right) rims.
TOP Testing the firmness of the netting with bamboo canes.

wiring the stem but just giving it a little extra hold and cannot be detected once the arrangement is completed.

There are various ways of fixing or holding wire netting firmly in place. Treating the whole container as though it were a parcel and tying the netting into position is the most elementary approach. This method is all right when using a shallow container, such as a large baking tin that is going to be placed where the container will be completely hidden. With such an arrangement it is a means of playing extra safe, and the telltale string can be hidden by materials coming well over the front; the string at the back of the vase can be secured to the window ledge for extra support and this will prevent the vase tipping over, as can so easily happen on a narrow ledge.

If string is used on a shallow container the flowers will almost certainly hide it when they are arranged. If the flowers are firm and well balanced the string can be cut away and they should stay in perfect position, but few people have the courage to do this!

A good idea is to use rubber bands—these can be bought in various colours and will seldom be seen if the arrangement is done well. They can be used for a jug, going round the top of the handle then over to the lip of the jug, and will be well hidden. Silver wire or fuse wire can also be used for tying the netting but it is rather more expensive.

If the container has an incurving rim you can place the netting under this then lift the central area up and it should remain firmly in place. On the other hand, if there is a rim to the outside of the vase, ears of netting can be pulled outwards and clipped over the rim, which will give a perfect hold.

It can be a problem to hide the mechanics in a glass goblet. Make a tangle of netting to fill the upper third of the vase, hooking the cut ends over the rim of the glass, and hide this with down-curving foliage, so that all the untidy netting and many of the stems are concealed.

If you use a valuable china vase or silver container, it is important to line it with thick brown paper or tin foil before attempting to place any wire netting in it. This will prevent scratching caused by sharp wire. Plastic-coated netting is easily available, although it is awkward to use as it is so thickly covered that it tends to move about in the vase and can only be firmly secured if it is tied with string. On the other hand, plastic-coated netting does last well because it does not rust.

In certain instances, wire netting can be successfully combined with a pinholder for extra weight. Similarly, it can be used in conjunction with plastic foam to soften the flow of the materials.

with a pinholder. Too large a piece will make it difficult to fit in all the stems, while too small a piece will move about in the container and inevitably the stems will move around too. The amount used will also depend on personal preference. I always like to fix my own so that it is just right for me. After a while you will know exactly how you like the netting, and then you are well on the way to a good arrangement.

To check the firmness of netting before arranging the flowers, it is a good idea to thread a few small pieces of bamboo canes through the mesh to see how well the layers of netting are placed in the container. Always place the cut ends of the netting in the top of the vase because they can be clipped round the vase handle or rim for extra security. Also, an awkward stem which moves round could have one of these cut ends carefully twisted round it. This is not

Pinholders

These are now available in many shapes and sizes and have become very popular. They are valuable for shallow containers and for flowers with thick stems where the elegance of the stems is of importance to the design of the arrangement.

Pinholders originated in Japan and consist of a heavy lead and alloy base into which sharp brass or steel pin-points have been set. As the pin-points may be of different lengths and distances apart, the right pinholder should be carefully chosen for the arrangement. It is a false economy to buy cheap pinholders because they will not last and are more expensive in the long run.

I seldom use a pinholder on its own—I prefer to use it in conjunction with a little wire netting so that support can be given to any thin-stemmed flowers which may be in the arrangement.

It is a tradition in England that the pinholder is always hidden, although this is not so in Japan. A little wire netting added to the vase eliminates the need to use any form of adhesive on the base of the pinholder, which is messy and unnecessary. When using pinholders, containers must be deep enough to hold at least 3·5 cm (1½ inches) of water if cut materials are to last for a reasonable length of time.

Keep pinholders dry when not in use, and do not force very thick woody material onto the pins without first splitting the material. You will only damage or bend the pins and weaken the holding capacity of the pinholder. The Oasis pinholder is another useful piece of equipment, and is particularly good for dried arrangements because it acts as a good balance for what can be a rather unstable arrangement in the weightless dry plastic foam.

Glass dome

For very heavy arrangements, the old-fashioned glass dome is worth considering. This does not normally suit home flower arrangements because flowers placed in ready-made holes have to stand in an upright position and it gives everything a 'surprised' look. The dome gives considerable weight to the vase, however, and if used in conjunction with netting for heavy materials such as stems of flowering cherry, this extra weight would be a great help. One or two of the upright stems can go through the netting into the glass dome, others can be threaded at the required angles through the netting and rest on top of the dome. A heavy pinholder could be used in just the same way though, and is far more versatile.

Sand and moss

Sand can be used to set little posies of flowers in small containers and is most effective when used on a flat round dish in which flower heads and petals have been set—a very formal type of arrangement, rather on the lines of a Victorian posy, which suits a low coffee table. Sand is heavy and inclined to scratch the surface of good china, so it should be used with care.

Moss is excellent for covering areas of soil in a planted dish or hiding an expanse of wire netting when arranging the first early Spring flowers in a copper pan or basket. It will give adequate support to a small group of flowers for a short period and, if kept moist, will maintain them without water. It is important to see that it is clean and free from any insect life before bringing it into the house. Always soak moss overnight in water before use.

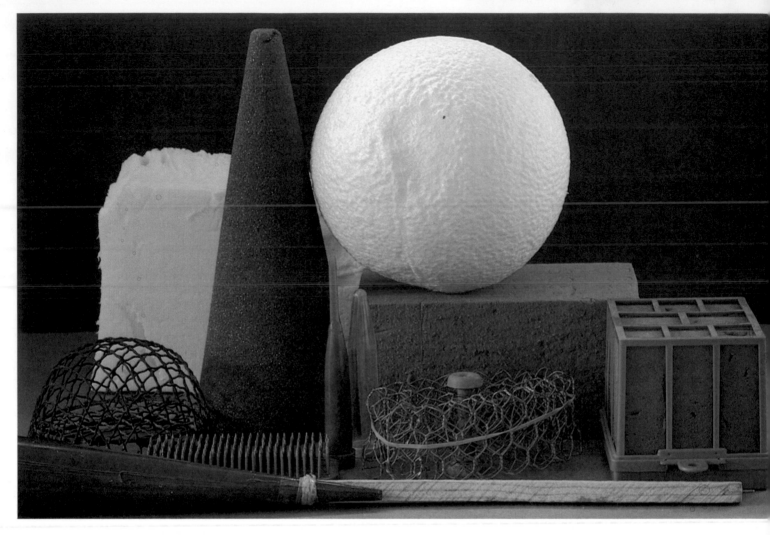

Plastic foam: Oasis, Mosy and Florapak

Water-retaining modern aids to flower arranging can be useful and certainly very many people like using them. For beginners, who do not seem to be happy with wire netting, plastic foam is good because stems will stay where they are placed and consequently give confidence to the arranger, but natural flowing lines are harder to achieve and the finished arrangement often has a rather stuffed look. Plastic foam encourages the use of straight stems placed at all angles to give very drooping sides and an exaggerated flow instead of curved-stemmed materials which would flow naturally over the edge of the vase rim. I would rather not use these aids except in a very small container with little room for netting. While they are essential for the florist whose arrangements have to be transported, I consider them an unnecessary extra expense for home use. Since flowers are often expensive, it seems better to forgo such extras and spend the money on the actual flowers.

Oasis and Mosy are plastic foam in block form or round units for posy bowls. They are generally used wet and this can be easily done by soaking them in a bucket for a few hours. They must then be kept wet. It is no use allowing them to dry then soaking them again. If the blocks are turned over and used from a different side, they can be used a few times but once they fall to pieces they should be discarded or completely broken up and used like Florapak, to hold stems in a container.

Some flowers are difficult to push into Oasis and little holes must first be made with a pencil so that when the stems are pressed into it they do not snap off. I also find that some flowers—anemones, for example—do not last well in it.

For use with dried materials, Oasis and Mosy should be used in their dry form.

Florapak has to be completely broken up and soaked in a bath of water until it becomes saturated. It is then packed into a bowl or container and covered with a little wire netting. The advantage of Florapak is that it is good for soft stems which will not penetrate Oasis, and it can be used a few times until it begins to smell. It is available in white and green.

time when working with artificial materials, but it should not be sprayed with aerosol paint sprays as these will dissolve it.

Flower tubes

To introduce a fresh flower stem to a bowl of growing plants, flower tubes can be used. They are often found attached to the stems of orchids which have come in from abroad. They are usually made from a plastic tube or phial with a rubber top. The stem is pushed straight through the rubber top into the water and the whole tube can then be set among the plants.

Flower cones

Made of metal or plastic, flower cones can be fixed to pieces of firm cane or, better still, square sticks which bite into the netting and remain firm in the container. They can be disguised with neutral green paint.

They hold flowers high in a very large group when their natural stems could not reach into the vase, and are used for special occasions such as weddings and large receptions.

Build up a framework of cones in the vase and arrange them in front of the background foliage, then group the flowers in the cones to make the overall arrangement look as natural as possible. A small tangle of netting may be useful in the cones, and they should be kept filled with water if the flowers are to last. It may be necessary to top them up twice a day if the room is very warm.

I am very much against the modern idea of building up great frameworks of cones and Oasis to get a large group from short-stemmed flowers. This is a nightmare to maintain afterwards and it is impossible to really get the same effect as that achieved with natural long-stemmed materials.

ABOVE Two blooms of *Paeonia* 'Sarah Bernhardt' are held in a thick glass goblet with polished stones which are both decorative and functional.

The Mazie

This is the brand name of a commercially produced flower holder which is an oval mass of small-mesh wire netting fitted with one or more suction cups. Some people find it useful for light arrangements of very thin-stemmed flowers, but it is not at all suitable for heavy groups of thick-stemmed flowers and branches, and ordinary wire netting secured in place will do the same job more cheaply.

Styrofoam

A hard cellulose material available in various shapes, styrofoam does not take up water and is used solely to hold mounted dry materials in place. It is useful at Christmas

Decorative stones

Pebbles, shells and marbles, lumps of polished crystal and even coal can all be used most effectively, not only to hold stems in glass containers, but also to camouflage ungraceful stalks, to conceal the pinholder and wire netting, or to form part of a garden on a dish.

Indeed, by choosing such accessories in colours which blend with your main colour scheme, and by using them with imagination in your container, you can greatly add to the beauty of your design. For example, try using small pieces of bright coal with aubergines, purple spray carnations, grapes and slate green-grey *Begonia rex* leaves on a pewter dish. See page 37 for an example of lumps of crystal used on a pewter dish.

47

The principles
of arrangement

PAGES 48–9 A well balanced arrangement picking up the colourings in the room. Note in particular the way the roses give 'weight' to the centre of the arrangement, and the materials radiate from a centre point with good down-flowing lines and 'break' (conceal) the rim of the vase. The materials in this white urn-shaped vase are *Rosa* 'New Dawn' and *R.* 'Virgo', *Digitalis, Achillea mollis, Escallonia longleyensis* and *Hosta glauca.*

General hints

Rules and regulations have no place in flower arranging and what will appeal to one person may well not please another, but there are a few helpful guidelines. Over-arranged flowers are not restful to the eye and the final arrangement should not be a true geometric shape; let simplicity and a natural look be your guide. You are creating a picture with your fresh flowers, container and background, just as an artist does with a canvas, paints and paint brush.

I always prefer to visualize the finished arrangement and build it up as I go along, rather than keep placing pieces of foliage and flowers together to create an arrangement. In fact, I first decide where a vase of flowers can stand, then I choose the container and work out the colours which would be suitable. From this point, with the arrangement in mind, I pick and collect the necessary materials, first the background material and sides, choosing pieces which are the correct shape and which curve in the right direction. Next I select something for the front of the vase, then the filling-in materials. In working this way, one tends not to over-pick—so many arrangements are spoilt from overcrowding, because once a material has been picked or bought it seems such a waste not to use it. I always think back to one of Constance Spry's favourite sayings: 'If in doubt, leave it out!'

⚓ Always use flowers in their various stages of development—buds, half-open flowers, and open flowers.

⚓ Flowers will need to be of different lengths—no two flowers of the same length should be next to each other. Have an 'in and out' effect rather than a flat level appearance.

⚓ Group the flowers into different shapes and colours and bring these through the arrangement in sweeps rather than in blocks of single colours.

⚓ Set the vase in the correct position before starting. If it has handles check that they are correctly positioned on either side when facing you. If it has a square base this should be absolutely square on when viewed from the front.

⚓ Try to arrange the flowers at the height at which they are to stand: by lowering or raising the vase you will get a different view of the flowers, so do the arrangement in the permanent position if you can.

⚓ Grade out the flowers into sizes, normally keeping the larger ones, especially the dark colours, to the centre. This does not necessarily apply once you have experience and a natural instinct for pleasing proportion and balance.

1

2

50

3

4

All stems should radiate from a centre point. Make use of curved stems, placing them in such a way that they flow from the container naturally. Flowers should not be mangled to conform to a geometric shape.

Always look at the flowers from the sides as well as at the front to see that they stand well in the vase.

Allow the flowers to flow over the rim of the vase, coming well out at the front.

Arrange the outline first and carefully prune out any unwanted pieces which make it appear too heavy. One or two stems should point slightly backwards to give the arrangement a less flat look and make all the difference to the vase.

Place the back stems about three quarters of the way across the vase for a facing arrangement. The area of wire netting at the back of these stems should be covered with a few short pieces of foliage to make it appear tidy and finished.

If you have only one or two flowers of a certain kind or colour, place them close together to give them more impact.

Avoid a 'surprised look' at all costs by always having a leaf or two to break the hard rim of the vase.

THIS PAGE Stages in the arrangement of a Summer basket.
1. *Polygonatum multiflorum, Paeonia* leaves and *Tellima grandiflora* set the height and width.
2. Three *Bergenia* leaves, radiating outwards, form the centre. *Camassia esculenta* and *Polygonum bistorta* are added.
3. Pink *Aquilegia* is added through the centre of the group and *Lonicera* is placed over the rim of the basket, to the left of the handle, to 'break' the hard rim of the container and link flowers and container together.
4. *Syringa vulgaris, S.* 'Preston' and *Paeonia* 'Madame Louis Henri' flowers are now added deep down, to give centre weight.
5. The finishing touches are made, making sure that the handle can be seen and, if necessary, be used to pick up the arrangement.

Colour

Formal theories of colour matching are based upon the position in the spectrum of the seven colours in the rainbow (red, orange, yellow, green, blue, indigo and violet), and colour theorists argue that certain combinations of colours are preferable to others. This may be so for certain purposes but in flower arrangement I have always found it advisable to discard any such preconceptions about colours.

Some people will go for bright, clear colours, others will favour the more subtle shades. Colour is an intensely personal affair about which it would be unwise to be dogmatic. Younger people often like bright colourings—for example, orange and blue together which is perfectly correct according to the colour wheel although I would rarely think of putting these two together. These rather hard colour combinations are often only fashionable for a short time and people soon tire of them, whereas one can live with the softer tones and shades for much longer.

On the other hand, to let personal prejudice prevent you from experimenting with possible colours is very limiting. We do not know whether everyone sees the same colours and I have often heard two people give different names to what seems to me to be the same colour. Try all colours in different combinations and see for yourself what effect they have. Different lights and backgrounds will change the colour effects. Keep an open mind and do not be ruled by the colour wheel. You may hit upon unexpectedly satisfactory results during your experiments. We have all heard such comments at a show as 'I should never have dared to put those two colours together but don't they look nice?'

Although we do not have rules about colour in flower arranging, some formal knowledge may be required, especially if you are going to enter the competition field.

Complementary colours are situated opposite each other on the colour wheel, such as yellow and violet, orange and blue, and red and green.

Analogous colours are situated next to each other. They are related, the primary colour dominating the other colour.

A **shade** is a colour with the addition of black.

A **tint** is a colour with the addition of white.

A **monochromatic** colour scheme is made up of tints and shades of one colour. It often causes some difficulty because a general colour such as pink can be dominated by blue pinks (such as the 'Carol' rose) or orange pinks (such as 'Doris' border carnations) and these do not really go together.

Greens are much loved by some, others find them dull and uninteresting and wish for a little colour to be added. The use of mixed greens relies largely on contrast of form, with different shapes next to each other—round leaves, sword-shaped leaves, fern fronds, ivy trails and so on. When assembling the material one looks for as wide a range of tones and shades as possible; pale, dark, grey-green, blue-green, yellow-green and variegated leaves. Constance Spry was particularly fond of mixed greens and introduced many interesting plants into arrangements which had never been used before. It was she who first used mixed greens for wedding bouquets.

Green groups have the advantage of lasting a long time and can easily be kept looking nice by replacing the odd leaf that dies. Green is a restful colour and suits most rooms. It is valuable in Summer as a contrast to the more brilliant Summer flowers in the garden. It has a toning-down effect when used with coloured flowers so should not be used for a really brilliant group.

Yellow tends to light up a mixed group of flowers and is particularly valuable during the long Winter months when there is little colour about. There is a wide range of yellows and the citron (greeny) yellow is a very popular colour with greens and mixed pastel shades.

Yellow and blue go well together: yellow and pink are not considered to do so, yet the beautiful rose 'Peace' is yellow, flushed with pink on the edges of its petals. I believe it is the way that colours are used that is of importance. Try to blend the yellow-cream and lime-green foliages such as hosta and elaeagnus with yellow flowers, so that the foliage complements the flower colour.

BELOW LEFT The colour wheel.
BELOW RIGHT This is a true clashing red arrangement. It stands in a copper bowl and contains a wide range of red colourings. The materials are *Rhus cotinus* 'Foliis purpureis', *Rosa rubrifolia, Prunus, Gladiolus, Atriplex hortensis rubra, Zinnia, Dahlia, Kentranthus, Geranium, Antirrhinum, Scabiosa, Amaranthus caudatus*.

Orange is a hard colour but, when mixed with browns, yellows and greens, can give very warm and striking effects. It is, perhaps, rather 'hot' for summer arrangements but lovely in the autumn, especially when arranged in copper and brass containers. Again, use foliages to bring out the colour.

Red is the colour for really magnificent effects and calls for courage when it is used. The wider the range of reds used, the better the result. It is fatal to weaken halfway—work through crimson, rose, ruby, vermilion, magenta, even orange. No single colour should stand out but the whole should light up with an exciting glowing note of red. Most, if not all, the green foliage should be cut out and red foliages such as prunus and beetroot, added instead.

Blue, although a lovely colour, can be difficult to use. It is not good under artificial light and may well be lost at night if used as a decoration for a dinner party. It can be absorbed by a background of grey stone walling and a large group used in a church can appear to have gaps in it from a distance if the blue flowers do not show up, so in such a position it needs a good background foliage. Blue colourings are cool in the day-time and look well in a mixed garden basket as a Summer decoration.

Pastel colours—soft pinks, blues, mauves, lavenders and creamy yellows—are always a delight when mixed with citron-green and grey foliages. They look well in most positions and seldom fail to please. They are perfect in soft grey china, grey-green coloured pewter and silver containers.

Mixed colours, when cleverly used can be lovely and one has only to study some of the Dutch masters' paintings to see this. It is always fun to try and make a Dutch group from a few stems of interesting materials. The best time for this is late Spring, or groups of mixed garden flowers in Summer.

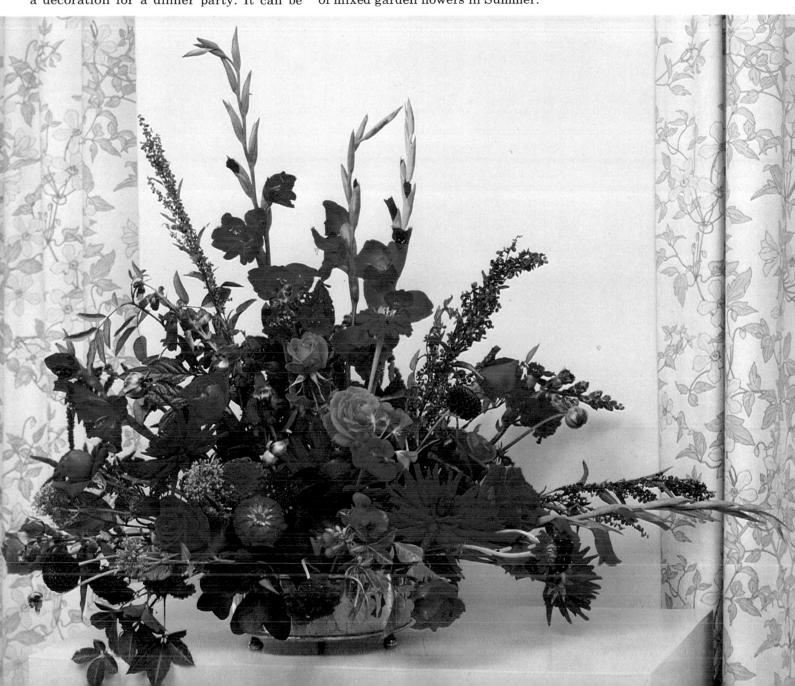

Room decoration

The use of flowers is an important aspect of interior decoration and the flower arrangements should form an integral part of the room. Some people contend that well-arranged groups of flowers, being beautiful in themselves, cannot look wrong, but the flowers should fit happily into their surroundings and not be too prominent.

It is of great importance to see a room first before deciding what to use in it. The colouring of the materials should relate to one of the main furnishing colours within that room. One room may call for reds while another may be so busy and colourful that just green and white is all that is required. Certain dye colours are not found in any growing material, so if the furnishing colours are difficult in this respect concentrate on complementing just one or two shades with flowers.

The position of flowers in the room is of the utmost importance and the best effect is generally achieved by concentrating on one or two large groups rather than having lots of little arrangements dotted about here and there as was done in Victorian times. On the other hand, I have seen a small cottage sitting room which had a few shelves on a wall and on these were many small arrangements of the most glorious flowers which looked as if they were pieces of china. It was quite beautifully done and very effective.

The personality of the room should control the flower decoration. The most important factor is the 'quality' of the room or some dominant feature, that is, its immediate impression, whether it is austere, dignified, simple, elaborate, pretty or 'modern'. A modern room, for example, may call for a simple line arrangement whereas the rather old-fashioned type of décor can take many more flowers in the arrangement. There will usually be some special feature in any room around which you may build your flower scheme; this may be a beautiful mirror or picture, an alcove, the wall colourings, or the colouring of the curtains or carpet.

Groups of flowers in a room usually look best when set against the solid background of a wall or a curtain with the light shining on them. They are most satisfactorily lighted from above by a spotlight or, if standing in an alcove, they can be lighted from above and behind with a warm light.

One of the most difficult tasks for the flower arranger is to plan flowers for a highly decorated room containing a lot of furniture. It may be necessary to provide a specially restful background. If you are working against a very strongly patterned wallpaper, a plain wall hanging could be positioned

BELOW These flowers and their container were chosen to match the dominant colourings in the room. The chrysanthemums are single stems of flowers and buds taken from three compound stems of florist's *Chrysanthemum* 'White Marble'. Other materials are *Hyacinthus, Scilla nutans* and *Eucalyptus*.

behind the flowers. This should harmonize with the wall colouring and can be in linen, shantung, hessian or a woven grass-cloth. Choose the right type of flowers for the background. Such specially contrived backgrounds are useful in difficult circumstances but they should be used with discretion because flowers always look best when they fit naturally with the rest of the room. Rich colours often look well in a book-lined room; they seem to associate well with the bindings, and elaborate vases can be used here to good effect.

Flowers should never be lit from below or stood on a glass base with a light in it: all this will do is to illuminate the mass of stems if using a glass container and also warm the flower water which may encourage breeding bacteria and create an unpleasant smell.

Certain flowers with translucent petals take on added glow and beauty when placed against the light. Iceland and Shirley poppies are a good example; they look particularly beautiful arranged against a window with the sun coming through them.

If flowers are being used to emphasize a particular decorative object in the room they should be placed near it; for instance, red flowers, designed to pick up the tones of a red picture, could be arranged below it in a low horizontal way; or the group could be

slender and pointed in shape and set at one side of the picture. In either case take care that the flowers or leaves do not obscure any part of the picture.

For smaller arrangements, various objects may be placed close by the flowers to complement them, such as a pewter platter, a polished copper tray, a piece of silver or a decorative china figure.

Flowers for a party are best placed on a mantelpiece where they are up out of the way and can be seen by all. Flowers on low tables on such an occasion are quite lost after the first few people have arrived. If the flowers are in front of a mirror, remember to tidy the back! Also, use fewer stems in the vase because mirrors tend to multiply the flowers.

Table flowers should be considered carefully. They should be simpler for a lunch than for an evening meal, both in their content and arrangement. For a special dinner, a candlestick may be suitable as the flowers would be lifted well off the table. Arrangements in candlesticks should be small, light and flowing and not have large flowers around the base of the candle as is so often seen. It is generally considered correct that table flowers should be low to allow a clear view across the table but this is not an infallible rule.

ABOVE The flowers arranged in this china urn pick up the colours of the painted flowers on it. They are *Malus floribunda, Primula vulgaris* and *P. denticulata, Alyssum saxatile, Muscari botrioides, Euonymus radicans variegatus.* The decorative copper kettle complements and enhances the arrangement.

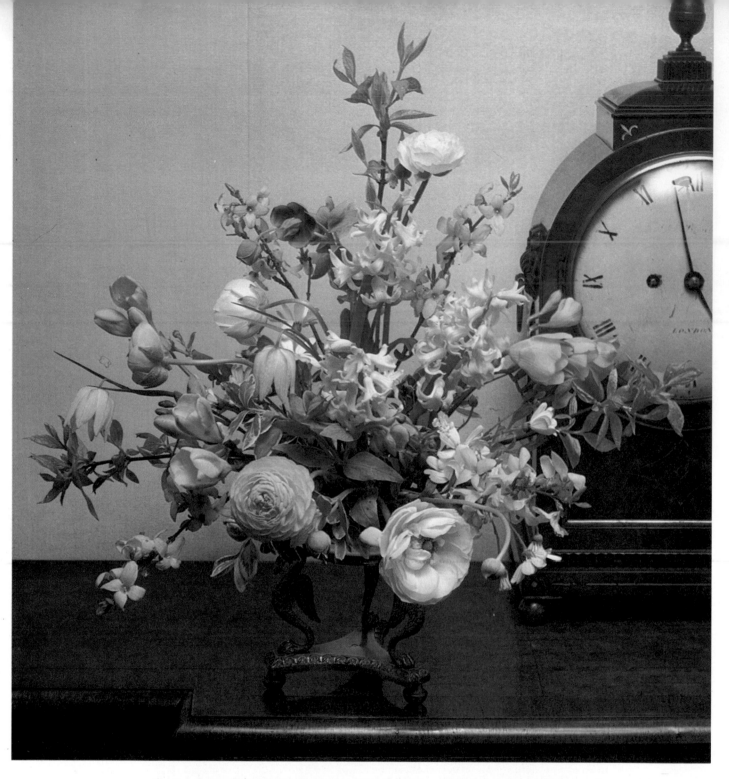

Spring is really the beginning of the flower arranger's year. By **March** gardens should be showing signs of change after the cold Winter. The extra daylight hours and higher temperatures encourage the buds to burst, only to be set back again by the occasional cold winds and frosts. Many of the Winter flowers and foliages will still be useful.

USEFUL MATERIALS
Azalea, Camellia, Cyclamen coum, Daphne mezereum, Echeveria retusa hybrida (from florist), *Iris tuberosa* syn. *Hermodactylus tuberosus, Lachenalia* (from florist), *Larix, Magnolia stellata, Muscari, Narcissi,*

Primula polyanthus, Primula vulgaris, Prunus, Ribes sanguineum, Viburnum.

Perhaps the best time of year for the flower arranger is **April**. It is then that there are so many interesting things available in the flower shops, gardens and the hedgerow.

USEFUL MATERIALS
Azalea, Betula, Camellia, Cineraria (from florist), *Erythronium dens-canis, Euphorbia, Fritillaria imperialis, Hosta, Hyacinthus, Lathyrus* (forced, from florist), *Magnolia soulangeana, Osmanthus delavayi, Primula, Rhododendron.*

May is often a good month for weather and a very big change takes place around the countryside. The majority of the trees are fully covered with fresh leaves and many are also in full flower during this month so this is a good time for big arrangements with large arching sprays of blossom.

USEFUL MATERIALS

Antirrhinum (from florist), *Arisarum*, *Centaurea*, *Convallaria majalis*, *Cytisus*, *Datura*, *Doronicum*, *Euphorbia*, *Fritillaria meleagris*, *Gentiana acaulis*, *Hydrangea* (from florist), *Matthiola*, *Myosotis*, *Polygonatum*, *Primula auricula*, *Ranunculus* (from florist), *Sorbus aria*, *Syringa*, *Trollius*, *Tulipa*, *Viburnum opulus sterile*.

PAGES 56–7

White forms of narcissi together with cowslips are simply arranged with foliages cut from the garden. The flowers are brought through the arrangement in groups for a more striking effect.

The white footed bowl is standing on a polished table and it is the reflection on the table and the way the light shows through the petals of the narcissi which emphasises the delicacy of the arrangement.

The use of flowers at all stages of their development is very important in flower arranging; note in particular the angular bud on the left hand side.

LEFT

The container for this arrangement is an old brass ink stand, in which a small glass bowl is placed to hold the wire netting, flowers and water.

Garden foliages provide the framework for the arrangement. A few cream cineraria have been used and they are the last of the flower heads from a plant whose foliage is no longer decorative at this time of year. The hyacinth stems are the secondary spikes from a pot of growing bulbs used for decoration just after Christmas. They looked untidy on the old bulbs, but cut and arranged here they have a new lease of life.

BELOW

This is a collection of short-stemmed Spring bits rather than an arrangement of any set pattern or shape. They have been placed in a shallow round bowl, making a useful table centre for a small dinner party. When only very little room is available the use of a small posy such as this is often very successful.

PAGES 56–7
Daphne pontica
Primula veris
Narcissus including
  'Actaea' and
  'Camellia'
Cymbidium
Callistemon

LEFT
Forsythia ovata
Philadelphus
Euonymus
Freesia
Ranunculus
Hyacinthus
Cineraria
Helleborus foetidus
Fritillaria meleagris

BELOW
Muscari latifolium
Hyacinthus
Primula vulgaris
Scilla
Dianthus
Narcissus

This shallow shell-edged oval vase makes an effective centre for a rectangular table. The container is so shallow that in addition to being fitted with wire netting, a small pinholder has been fixed in the centre.

The soft silver-grey lamb's tongues have been used before any flowers have formed and this gives them extra stem length. Care must be taken to see that the thick felty leaves are always held above the water level as they readily syphon water from the vase.

The sharp lime-green flower heads of euphorbia have been brought up through the arrangement from side to side.

The arrangement is completed with pale-coloured cultivated bluebells. Cultivated bluebells have rather stiff thick fleshy stems and wild ones would probably have created a softer effect; they would certainly have been a deeper shade.

RIGHT

This pleasing arrangement stands in a shallow grey fluted fruit bowl. Wide variegated aspidistra and large artichoke leaves at the base give way to narrow spiky foliage at the top. All the stems flow from a centre point and this is emphasized by the deep purple grapes giving extra weight at the centre. The English iris have been chosen for their colour which complements the grapes.

The flowers are held in position by wire netting and a pinholder, and the stem of the grapes has been hooked into the wire at the rim of the vase.

BELOW RIGHT

Two bunches of mixed wallflowers are arranged in a hamper basket. The lid has been propped up with a short length of cane and contributes to the cottage-style effect of the arrangement. Wallflowers look well in simple containers. They are usually more effective when arranged on their own and here the stems have all been cut to different lengths for variety rather than a flat mass of flowers. Stems should be hammered and all foliage below the water line must be removed as the wallflower is a member of the cabbage family and the water will quickly start to smell.

Wallflowers are not long lasting but they offer a wealth of colour and a lovely scent.

RIGHT
Cynara scolymus
Tulipa
Rhododendron
Erica
Lamium
Iris xiphioides
Ixia
Senecio greyii
Hedera
Pelargonium
Aspidistra elatior
  variegata
Helleborus orientalis
Eucalyptus gunnii

BELOW
Scilla nutans
Stachys lanata
Euphorbia cyparisias

BELOW RIGHT
Cheiranthus

Step-by-step arrangement

1. Whitebeam is an excellent background foliage because it has such well-shaped branches. Here its silvery green foliage looks well against the pale green background. It needs a good firm anchorage as the branches are heavy and for this arrangement a wide bowl has been used, containing a heavy pin-holder and a mass of wire netting raised well above the vase rim for extra support.

The stems all radiate from a centre point and flow well over the vase rim. Provided the vase is kept full, stems positioned horizontally have access to as much water as those standing upright.

2. Six stems of double cherry are added next and they too flow from a centre point and look comfortable.

3. Five stems of euphorbia and a few artichoke leaves complete the arrangement, giving weight to the centre of the vase.

The container is no longer visible and only serves the purpose of holding water and anchoring the stems.

Sorbus aria lutescens
Prunus serrulata
  'Kansan'
Euphorbia characias
Cynara scolymus

62

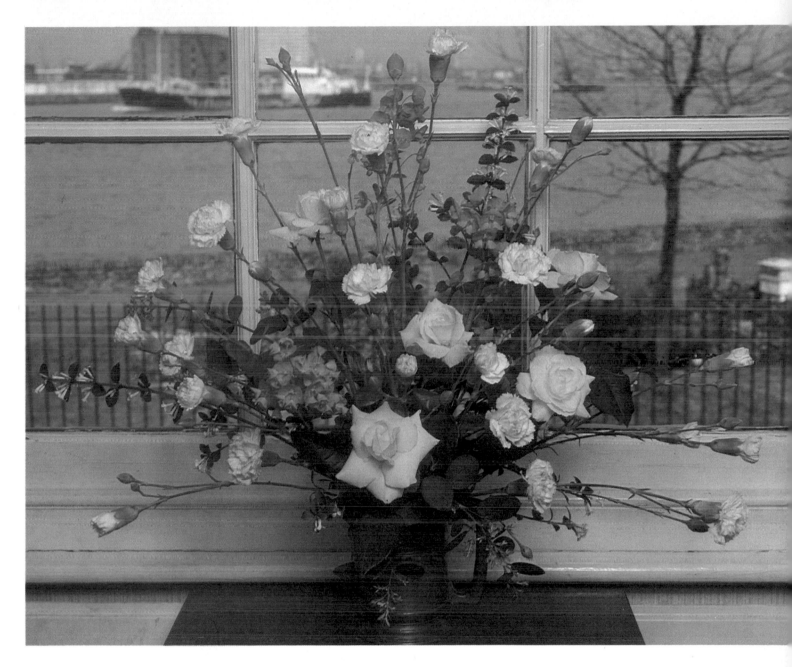

Small arrangements of mixed green foliages can be made at any time of the year. All the foliages and seed heads for this arrangement came from my small city garden except for a few cuttings from houseplants.

The vase is made from a real shell fixed to a dolphin base. It is quite small (compare its size with the paperbacks on the shelf above) so the stems are held in a little block of Oasis to allow them to flow at angles from the shell yet still receive moisture.

ABOVE
So often in Spring yellow flowers are from the narcissus family, but here is a pint-sized pewter tankard containing small yellow roses and spray carnations which are yellow flecked with pink. These florist's flowers are the sort of flowers one might receive as a gift purchased from a flower shop, and for the arrangement they have been supplemented with garden foliage. The carnations are used at various stages of development and the buds will open out in the arrangement.

LEFT
Geranium
Helleborus
Hedera
Asparagus meyerii
Zantedeschia
Osmanthus
Erica
Ruta graveolens
Passiflora caerulea
Veronica
Euonymus

ABOVE
Eucalyptus gunnii
Osmanthus delavayi
Rosa 'Spanish Sun'
Dianthus
Euphorbia robbiae

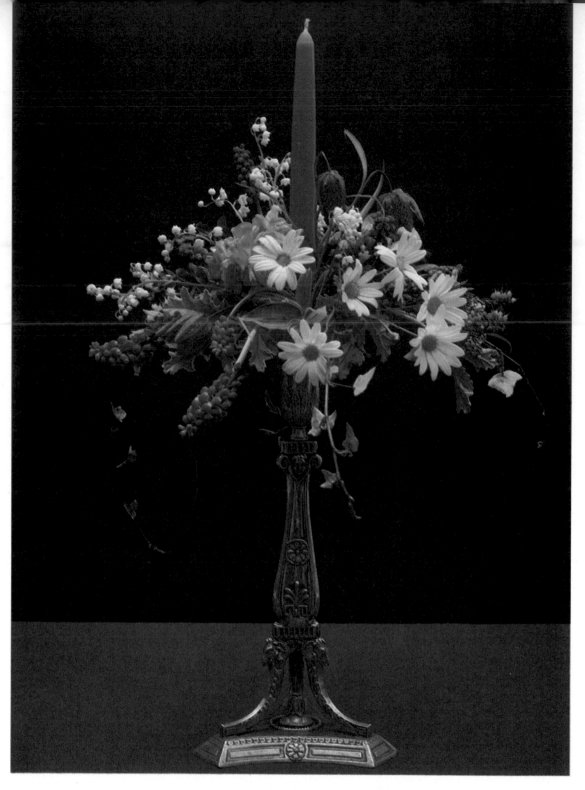

ABOVE

Muscari

Convallaria majalis

Erica

Fritillaria meleagris

Geranium

Pulmonaria angustifolia

Chrysanthemum
  leucanthemum

Hedera

Tradescantia

Pieris japonica

Ajuga atropurpurea
  variegata

ABOVE

This sophisticated table centre for a dinner party is arranged in a silver candlestick fitted with an aluminium candle cup. The candle cup was originally designed in glass by Constance Spry to hold flowers at a dinner given by government ministers for Her Majesty The Queen.

The materials are arranged in wire netting and flow gracefully over the edge of the candle cup. The flower stems have been cut quite short and the flowers are grouped together rather than dotted about to make a greater impact.

RIGHT

This cheerful Springtime arrangement of daffodils and narcissi with mixed foliage gives a pleasing decoration for a cottage dining room.

Daffodils are difficult to arrange and need to face in all directions to look natural. Simple containers suit them and here a rectangular basket completes the rustic effect and complements the simple style of the dining room.

Viburnum foliage with small flower sprays has been used to fill in the base of the arrangement and hide the netting.

Not all bluebells are blue, and here pink, white and blue cultivated bluebells have been used in equal quantities. They were arranged in the vase first and then the bare stems were filled in with small pieces of euphorbia.

Euphorbia and bluebells are both extremely useful Spring garden materials and they go well together for simple arrangements.

The container for this arrangement is a round frosted-glass bowl, but as it is an all-round arrangement for a low wooden table the vase is hardly visible.

BELOW	RIGHT
Narcissus	*Scilla nutans*
Salix	*Euphorbia robbiae*
Corylus	
Viburnum tinus	

Summer

June immediately conjures up roses in the minds of flower arrangers. Many flowers and foliages are very prolific in this month and the decorator has a great choice.

USEFUL MATERIALS

Alchemilla, Astrantia, Centaurea cyanus, Delphinium, Dianthus, Digitalis, Eremurus, Escallonia, Geranium, Lilium, Lupinus, Nigella, Paeonia, Papaver, Passiflora caerulea, Philadelphus, Pyrethrum, Rosa, Spartium junceum, Tilia.

The months of **July** and **August** normally see a change in the overall flower colourings in the garden. Brighter colours creep in as many mixed annuals are now in flower. Towards the end of August one should start to select materials for drying and preserving for the Winter months ahead.

USEFUL MATERIALS

Achillea, Angelica, Chrysanthemum, Delphinium, Echinops, Eryngium, Lathyrus, Lilium, Nicotiana, Phlox, Rosa, Salvia, Scabiosa, Solidago, Veratum nigrum.

PAGES 68–9

A glorious collection of old-fashioned garden roses in the drawing room at Constance Spry's own home in Berkshire. The container is a Dresden china fruit dish, lined with a simple white china bowl.

ABOVE

A pretty pink Wedgwood powder bowl is the container for this delicate arrangement of short-stemmed flowers. Sweet peas and roses have a pleasing perfume, making this a delightful arrangement for a bedroom. The lid is propped up with a length of cane, and a small piece of Oasis holds the flowers.

RIGHT

This white double rose has a lovely scent and makes an attractive table setting when simply arranged with its own foliage. Great care is needed when using glass containers to ensure that the mechanics do not show and the water is clean.

PAGES 68–9

Rosa 'Charles de Mills'
  'Cardinal Richelieu'
  'Madame Ernst Calvat'
  'Madame Isaac Pereire'
  'Belle de Crécy'
  'Constance Spry'

ABOVE

Rosa 'Jenny Wren'
Lathyrus
Alchemilla

RIGHT

Rosa 'Alba Maxima'

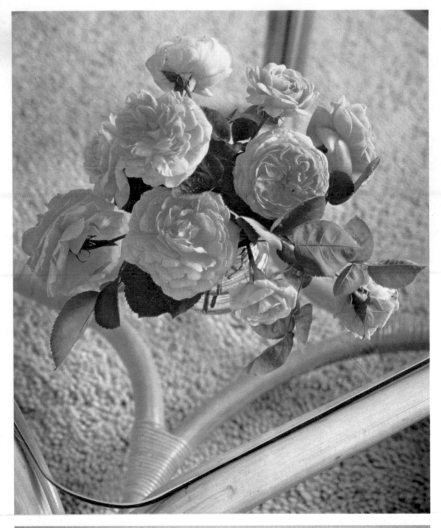

The rose named after Constance Spry has a lovely muddled centre and a delightful scent. It is very heavy when fully open and tends to hang over like an open paeony. Unfortunately it only flowers during June for a short period and there is no second crop in early Autumn.

The flowers are arranged to be viewed from above as they are standing on a low glass-topped coffee table.

RIGHT

Sweet peas are available in such an attractive range of colours that their success in an arrangement is often the result of a careful choice of colours. Here they have been chosen to complement the décor of the room which is predominantly blue.

Green alchemilla, dotted throughout the arrangement provide an interesting contrast to the sweet peas. Only a few alchemilla leaves are needed to break the rim of the vase at the front and soften the harsh angular look of the container. Care must always be taken when using silver containers as their bright shine can easily conflict with the delicacy of flowers.

BELOW RIGHT

The soft grey colour of this alabaster tazza tones well with the pink flowers and green-grey eucalyptus foliage. As the bowl is very shallow the flowers are arranged in a glass dish on a pinholder with a little wire netting.

Antirrhinums and the buds of Doris border carnations make the outline for this triangular-shaped arrangement. Euonymus runs through it from the left and the large well-marked arum leaf gives added weight to the centre.

LEFT

Even a small bunch of border carnations can make a successful room decoration. Here they are arranged in a half-pint pewter tankard. The stems are cut to different lengths to give variety and depth to the arrangement, and the flowers' own foliage, buds and shoots add interest.

ABOVE LEFT	RIGHT
Rosa 'Constance Spry'	*Antirrhinum*
	Dianthus × *allwoodii*
ABOVE RIGHT	'Doris'
Lathyrus	*Dianthus* 'Pink Jim'
Alchemilla mollis	*Euonymus latifolius*
	variegatus
LEFT	*Helleborus orientalis*
Dianthus × *allwoodii*	*Arum italicum pictum*
'Doris'	*Viburnum carlesii*
	Eucalyptus gunnii
	Rosa 'Carol'

ABOVE RIGHT
Sorbus aria
Cynara scolymus
Digitalis
Lupinus
Allium
Matthiola
Syringa 'Preston'
Rhododendron ponticum
Rosa 'Magenta'

RIGHT
Escallonia 'Apple Blossom'

ABOVE

The corner of a room is often a good place in which to stand flowers as they show up well yet are out of the way. This arrangement has been made to suit the shape of the recessed wall and look comfortable in its surroundings without appearing contrived.

The pewter measure container not only suits the colour of the flowers, but its heavy nature helps it to take the 'height' of the materials in it. Substantial-looking flowers such as these would look quite unbalanced in a delicate container.

RIGHT

Just five shapely stems of escallonia in a narrow-necked coffee pot constitute this elegant arrangement. Choose thin-stemmed branches in preference to thick-stemmed pieces when using a narrow-necked vase as you will be able to fit in more pieces. Always remember to let the natural shape of the branch dictate its positioning – a straight piece forced to curve over the side of the container will never look happy. Compare this with the step-by-step arrangement of white-beam branches on page 62.

BELOW

A tall mantelpiece is a good place on which to stand flowers, especially for a party, as they are well out of reach yet easily seen.

The container for this arrangement of mixed reds is a shallow mirror trough. Being long and low it is well suited to a mantelpiece position. Note the way in which the three compound heads of roses have been used in the centre, giving weight and depth of colour, while the single-headed stems of the sweet williams are on the outside. The foliage adds flowing lines to the arrangement.

BOTTOM

Old-fashioned roses look best when simply arranged with their own foliage (see also pages 71 and 72). Here just two varieties are used: the climbing 'La Follette' is the pink rose and 'Blanc Double de Coubert' is the white. This was the rose chosen by Constance Spry for a decoration in the retiring room for H.M. the Queen straight after her coronation when a simple basket was filled to overflowing with this sweet-smelling white rose. The flowers are used in various stages of development and will open out.

ABOVE RIGHT
Rosa 'Rosemary Rose'
Dianthus barbatus
Symphoricarpos

RIGHT
Rosa 'Blanc Double de
    Coubert'
Rosa 'La Follette'

This is not quite a clashing red arrangement (see page 53) as a few green rhododendron leaves have been used to break the rim of the vase, and the crab apple has some green colouring. Nevertheless it achieves a similarly stunning effect, enhanced by the rich shiny surface of the inlaid table.

ABOVE
Malus atrosanguinea
Syringa
Bergenia cordifolia
  purpurea
Rhododendron
Geranium cerise
Tulipa

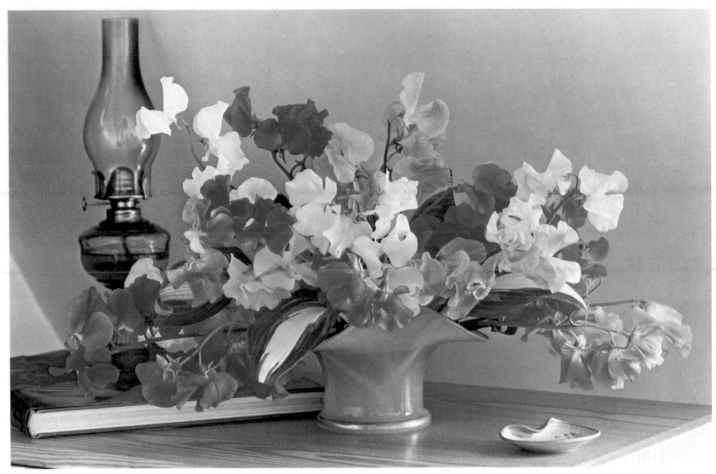

ABOVE

As sweet peas have a rather fussy outline, a clear-cut foliage such as hosta complements them well. Compare this arrangement of sweet peas with that on page 73 where alchemilla was used giving a dotted effect to the arrangement.

RIGHT

The warm colour of this arrangement is unusual for Summer but it would be a good decoration for a cool evening. Note how the weight of colour from the orange lily is kept to the centre of the vase and the lighter colours flow in sweeps outwards from the centre. The yellow ivy foliage used at the base of this arrangement is a useful plant for the flower arranger to grow if a little wall space is available.

FAR RIGHT

This marble and alabaster vase lends itself to arrangements with flowing lines where each leaf and flower is placed in a very clear-cut position. The lines of the arrangement tie up with the lines of carving on the rim and stem of the vase. This is a good style of arrangement to show off materials of special interest. Here the five clematis are the focal point even though they are not centrally placed.

LEFT
Lathyrus
Hosta undulata

BELOW
Cordyline purpurea
Gladiolus
Allium oiculum
Alchemilla mollis
Achillea 'Moonshine'
Lilium pyrenaicum
Lilium 'Enchantment'
Rosa 'Golden Rain'
Rosa 'Pitica'
Antirrhinum
Hedera
Lonicera
Kalanchoe
Anemone pulsatilla
Muscari
Euonymus japonicus
    albo-marginatus
Elaeagnus pungens
    'Aureo-Maculata'

ABOVE
Heuchera
Clematis florida
    'Bicolor'

Geranium crispum
    variegatum
Geranium 'Golden
    Harry Hieover'

Echeveria retusa
Begonia cleopatra
Sedum sieboldii variegata
Lunaria biennis

Rosa chinensis viridis
Iris foetidissima
Asparagus meyerii
Ballota pseudodictamnus

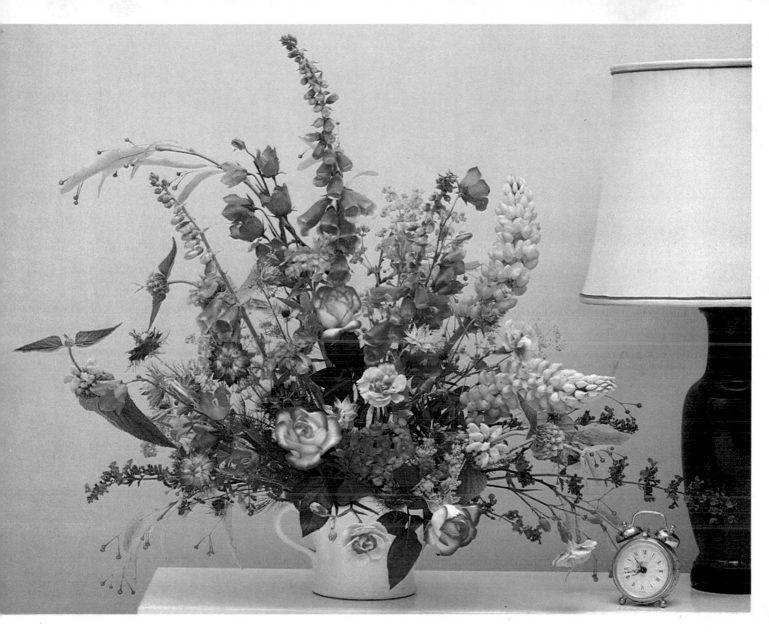

LEFT

Branches of stripped lime make a very attractive background foliage. Make sure that every leaf is stripped off the branches so the bracts show clearly and to good effect. The three artichoke leaves at the centre of the vase help to link the container and the flowers. The stripped lime and lilies, which have a tendency to look rather light and airy, would otherwise be out of keeping with the heavy vase.

The colour of the paeonies, dotted through the arrangement, picks up the pink of the lily buds.

ABOVE

A heavy white ceramic vase with a handle each side holds a collection of mid-Summer flowers picked from a herbaceous border, together with a few side shoots of stripped lime and three commercial roses.

The lupins which have been filled with water and plugged are now beginning to take up natural curves.

FAR RIGHT
This is an all round arrangement for a low coffee table. It stands in a shallow pewter fruit dish containing a dome of wire netting. The colourings, which include a whole range of pink and mauve tones, have been chosen to blend in with the predominant colouring of the furnishing fabric. Although many of these tones may be said to clash, the overall effect is a good blend. See also the clashing red arrangement on page 53. A few extra leaves at the centre make up for the lack of foliage on such stems as the annual scabious.

BELOW
A bold all-round arrangement of red and white roses, chosen to carry through the colour scheme of the room. The flowers are simply arranged with plenty of their own foliage in a white tazza.

BELOW RIGHT
Fruit always adds importance to a group of flowers and here is a splendid group of flowers and fruit arranged in a copper pan. This would be a very suitable decoration for a sideboard or buffet table at a party.

The netting has been kept high to support the fruit and a heavy pinholder has been placed at the centre-back of the container to weight the pineapple. The pineapple itself has a piece of cane pushed into it to give it the necessary height. The grapes have been kept in their bunches and bedded down on a few leaves to stop them getting tangled in the netting.

The flowers are arranged in the usual way, flowing from a centre point. The exotic torch lily, *Gloriosa*, is a climbing lily which is easy to grow in a greenhouse and very long lasting.

RIGHT
Hydrangea
Dahlia
Anemone
Spiraea douglassii
Scabious
Delphinium
Phlox
Senecio
Artemesia

BELOW
Rosa 'Paul's Scarlet'
Rosa 'Iceberg'

BELOW
Cordyline purpurea
Polygonatum multiflorum
Smilacina racemosa
Rhododendron 'Ghent'
Gloriosa rothschildiana
Iris pseudacorus
Lilium 'African Queen'
    and *L. pyrenaicum*
Gerbera
Euphorbia palustris and
    E. robbiae
Aralia
Allium siculum

Autumn

The rich colours of Autumn make a glorious display. The container for this arrangement is a plastic plant saucer standing on a flat round basket and the stems are arranged in Oasis with just a single layer of wide-mesh netting over the top to help achieve a flowing arrangement. The flowering hops flow attractively over the edge of the shelf.

A simple arrangement can quickly brighten up a narrow dark hallway. Here just five rudbeckia flowers and a little osmanthus foliage make a practical upright arrangement in a modern cylindrical pottery vase. The osmanthus softens the rather severe lines of the rudbeckia stems which have very little foliage of their own.

PAGES 84–5
Gladiolus
Dahlia
Helianthus
Azalea (foliage)
Symphoricarpos
Humulus
Begonia
Solidago
Kniphofia
Cactus
Nicotiana
Chrysanthemum

LEFT
Rudbeckia
Osmanthus

Nicotiana
Ligustrum vulgare
Eucalyptus
Dahlia 'Pompom'
Chrysanthemum
Calendula
Helianthus
Matthiola

September is the month of dahlias and the Michaelmas daisy. Dahlias are heavy flowers so arrangements are often fairly large.

USEFUL MATERIALS
Agapanthus, Amaranthus, Aster, Brassica, Chrysanthemum, Clematis vitalba, Cobaea, Crinum, Dahlia, Eucomis, Euonymus europaeus, Freesia (from florist), *Gentiana sino-ornata, Gladiolus* (from florist), *Humulus, Phlox, Phytolacca, Reseda, Rosa, Veratum nigrum, Verbena, Vitis, Zinnia.*

The Autumnal colourings are enhanced by the appearance of fruit and berries in **October**. The intensity of the Autumnal tint varies annually, being far more colourful in a dry Autumn.

USEFUL MATERIALS
Achillea, Aster, Chrysanthemum, Colchicum, Dahlia, Delphinium, Hydrangea, Nerine, Rosa, Rudbeckia, Zinnia.

ABOVE
Often a few leftover pieces from larger arrangements can make an ideal group for a small occasional table. Here, for example, the fine-leaved eucalyptus stems are the basal side shoots removed from larger stems, and there are short stems of calendula and chrysanthemum. The use of some chrysanthemum buds helps to keep the arrangement from looking too heavy. The berries are from privet in its early green stage: when black, two or three months later, they are very useful in Winter groups.

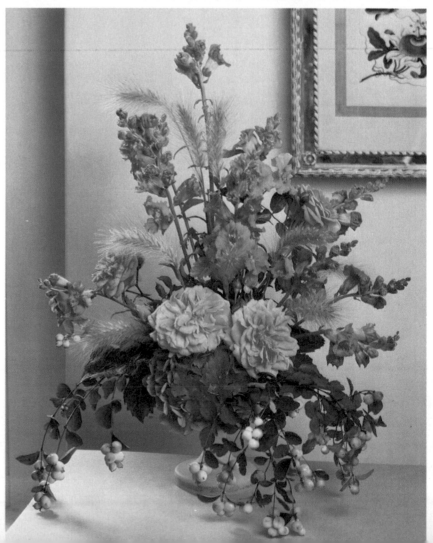

ABOVE

The pure white Autumn crocus is less common than the purple variety but it is delightful when arranged with just a few other flowers. The pompom dahlias are off-white with pink backs to their petals, picking up the colour of the freesia buds. The open freesia links up with the two annual scabious, and a bunch of elderberries gives weight to the centre of the group. Variegated ivy is the backing foliage.

RIGHT

This attractive arrangement makes use of a range of pink tones, offset by a little green, for its effect. The snapdragons and grass heads make the height of the arrangement while the snowberries, tinged with pink, break the rim of the vase. The two semi old-fashioned roses and a hydrangea head give weight to the centre.

ABOVE	RIGHT
Colchicum	*Antirrhinum*
Hedera	*Symphoricarpos*
Dahlia 'Pompom'	*Rosa* 'Dream Girl'
Scabious	*Hydrangea*
Sedum	*Pennisetum*
Lathyrus	
Freesia	
Sambucus	
Polygonum	

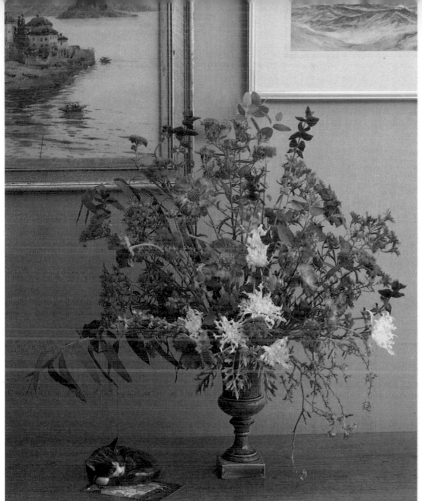

LEFT

A formal urn-shaped vase generally calls for an arrangement with clean-cut materials, but here the setting, dominated by the colourings of the paintings, suits this group even though the flowers have a rather fussy outline. The white chrysanthemum is a delicate American spray which is very useful because it breaks down well into many side shoots for easy arranging. The seakale is wild, collected from the seashore.

BELOW

A wide range of containers is an important asset to the flower arranger. This shallow shell dish with a little cherub perched at one end is in fact a soap dish! The flowers are short in the stem so just the stem tips are threaded through a small ball of wire netting held under the cherub's feet.

LEFT	BELOW
Scabious	*Anemone* 'The Bride'
Salvia	*Gentiana sino-ornata*
Aster	*Rosa* 'Cecile Brunner'
Ageratum	*Eucalyptus*
Crambe	*Cineraria*
Chrysanthemum 'Crystal'	
Senecio cineraria	
Eucalyptus	

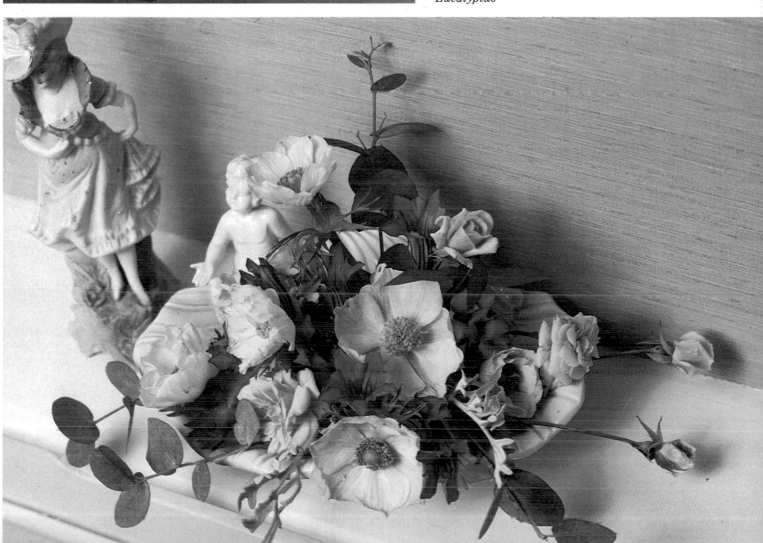

RIGHT

This arrangement was created to fit neatly on a mirrored window sill. The stems, arranged in a block of Oasis standing in a flat dish, flow from a centre point following the lines of the walls.

FAR RIGHT

It is always important to arrange flowers in relation to their setting. Here there is a strong Chinese influence so a papier-mâché Chinese bowl (with a metal lining) contains a few exotic materials such as the swan plant, which resembles bamboo foliage.

BELOW

This small arrangement of Autumn greens in a china shell vase shows up some of the many different shapes available in materials at this time of year. The pretty calyx of cobaea can be used after the bell-shaped flower has fallen and it is very long-lasting.

RIGHT
Molucella
Lonicera
Helianthus

BELOW
Cobaea scandens
Symphoricarpos
Euonymus
Tellima
Hedera
Polygonum

FAR RIGHT
Amaryllis
Bergenia
Sedum
Paeony (foliage)
Asclepias physocarpa

ABOVE

The pompom, single and cactus varieties of dahlias are grouped together here to give a splash of colour in a dark area at the foot of a staircase. Having such large flower heads, dahlias tend to make arrangements look rather heavy so here sloe foliage and some dahlia buds are used to help lighten the group.

RIGHT ABOVE

This two-arm pottery candlestick makes a good table centre for a rectangular table. It holds two aluminium candlecups which have been painted to match the candlestick. A small amount of netting has been placed in each, and for extra security the netting is taped to the candlecups with Oasis tape, as some of the materials used are quite heavy and could make the arrangement topple.

RIGHT

An all-round arrangement of mixed anemones is bright and colourful. This arrangement was made from two small bunches (twenty-four stems) and as there were only a few white flowers these have been grouped together to make them show up to advantage. Note the fact that no two flowers of the same length are next to each other and that some are placed deep down in the centre of the arrangement. Most of the greenery comes from the feathery collars of the anemones.

Anemones are normally at their best during the Autumn, Winter and Spring but their quality is very dependent on the weather. During a wet cold spell they can be short in the stem, their petals are often damaged and they do not last well when cut. Limp flowers can often be revived with a little hot water.

ABOVE
Dahlia
Prunus spinosa

RIGHT ABOVE
Rubus
Sambucus
Cobaea scandens
Rosa 'Carol'
Colchicum
Astrantia
Hedera

RIGHT
Anemone
Hedera
Eucalyptus

Zinnias are one of those flowers which look best arranged on their own with just a little foliage to give the arrangement some shape. The foliage of zinnia itself is rather uninteresting so here Autumn-tinted azalea and osmanthus foliage is used.

This group of baby zinnias in a copper jelly mould makes a striking arrangement on a shining brass table top. The large-flowered zinnias can be difficult to arrange as they sometimes bend over just below the flower head and may need supporting with a wire up the hollow stem.

If you have just a few of a particularly interesting material it is often best to use them on their own rather than in a mixed arrangement. The full beauty of these five hybrid nerine shows up well in this tall arrangement. Nerine are rarely picked with their own foliage so here black water grass was used to give the required height and lightness, and as the grass is light it will not upset the balance of the tall cylinder vase. A couple of trails of ivy hide the small ball of netting at the top of the vase and enhance the flow of the arrangement.

RIGHT

This elegant arrangement gives a good show of Autumn colour. The height is made from a single stem of atriplex and is linked to the rest of the group by many stems of various shades of kniphofia and a few salpiglossis in bronze shades. Dahlias and roses give weight to the vase and megasea leaves link the flowers to the container. Note the way the kniphofia have taken up flowing lines in water.

ABOVE	RIGHT
Nerine	*Atriplex hortensis rubra*
Hedera	*Kniphofia*
Gramineae	*Salpiglossis*
	Dahlia
LEFT	*Rosa* 'Vesper'
Zinnia	*Rosa* 'Brownie'
Azalea	*Megasea*
Osmanthus	*Tricholaena rosea*

Very little foliage has been used in this simple collection of yellow garden flowers in order to make the group show up well against the dark background.

BELOW
This bright flower group stands on a wall table in a hallway, striking a cheerful note of welcome. It is arranged in an Oasis tray and picks up the colour and texture of the wallpaper. The flowers used are quite simple but the strength of colour is greater for the lack of green foliage—in fact a few rose leaves are the only green leaves in the arrangement. The roses and antirrhinums have been carefully placed at the centre to give weight to the arrangement.

LEFT
Lilium 'Destiny'
Rudbeckia
Antirrhinum
Helianthus
Alstroemeria
Gladiolus
Kniphofia
Solidago
Hedera
Achillea

BELOW
Statice sinuata
Solidago
Antirrhinum
Gladiolus
Atriplex
Amaranthus caudatus
 'Viridis'
Rosa 'Golden Showers'

Winter

November sees the end of most of the colour in the garden and it is always a shame that the last blossoms tend to go over very quickly in the warmth of a heated house. But there are many interesting materials available during the Winter months if only one looks carefully around—the first flowers of *Jasminum nudiflorum*, the buds of *Helleborus orientalis* tucked deeply in the foliage, and the early *Narcissus* 'Paper White' and *N.* 'Soleil d'Or' appear in the flower shops.

USEFUL MATERIALS
Berberis, Cotoneaster, Chrysanthemum (from florist), *Erica, Ilex, Mahonia, Narcissus* (from florist), *Prunus subhirtilla autumnalis, Pyracantha, Viburnum fragrans.*

December can be a very colourful month inside the home but the garden tends to be less so. Many of the berries will be lost to the birds and the flower arranger must look to the different shapes and tones of green in plant materials, instead of relying on colour from flowers. Artificial materials are often introduced at Christmas time and can be very attractive if used thoughtfully, following the usual principles of arrangement.

USEFUL MATERIALS
Arbutus unedo, Garrya elliptica, Helleborus niger, Hyacinthus, Iris stylosa, Jasminum nudiflorum, Viburnum fragrans.

SPECIAL CHRISTMAS MATERIALS
Cedrus atlantica glauca, Elaegnus aureo variegata, Hedera, Ilex, Picea pungens, Taxus baccata, Tsuga canadensis, Viscum album.

January is usually still a sparse time for garden flowers and only a few hardy ones will venture out. However, the change of seasons does vary greatly year by year, depending on the weather, and in some years in the south a camellia may be in full flower by mid-January.

USEFUL MATERIALS
Azalea, Corylus, Eranthis hyemalis, Galanthus nivalis, Hamamelis mollis, Hyacinthus, Iris unguicularis stylosa, Narcissus (from florist), *Salix caprea.*

February can be another difficult month but more and more flowers are available in the shops and these can be happily supplemented by garden foliages.

USEFUL MATERIALS
Alnus, Chimonanthus fragrans, Cornus mas, Crocus, Forsythia, Pieris floribunda, Syringa (from florist), *Tulipa, Viburnum opulus sterile* (from florist).

PAGES 98–9
Winter need not be a scant time for arrangements in the home. All the foliage and berries used in the arrangement on the previous page were found growing wild in the hedgerow in December.

ABOVE
Winter jasmine flowers throughout the Winter and here the first few stems are grouped with those other useful Winter materials, viburnum and alder.

A stem of alder, cut and placed in water, will easily last for two months indoors and the catkins will grow and become very decorative. The bare branches just lightly covered with glitter can also make a useful Christmas decoration.

RIGHT
Large chrysanthemum blooms are one of the few flowers readily available from florists during the Winter months and it is often difficult to use a small bunch of these. Here just five flowers are simply arranged. A stem of alder fitted to a pinholder makes the height and two side shoots form the width.

PAGES 98–9
Crataegus oxycantha
Symphoricarpos
Rosa canina
Ligustrum vulgare
Rhamnus cathartica
Euonymus europaeus
Hedera
Mahonia

ABOVE
Jasminum nudiflorum
Myrtus
Alnus
Viburnum fragrans

RIGHT
Chrysanthemum 'Yellow Indianapolis'
Aucuba japonica
Alnus

LEFT

A useful Winter arrangement can be made from small pieces of many different garden foliages. This type of mixed green arrangement does not call for particular materials to be grouped together or for one material to flow through the group. Instead, the aim should be to get different shapes and colours next to each other to enable each piece to show to good advantage.

RIGHT

Another useful and long-lasting arrangement for the Winter can be made using houseplants grouped purposefully together in a trough. Often a collection of houseplants is just thrown together without any thought given to the normal principles of flower arrangement, concerning, for example, the height and width of the arrangement and the shape of the individual materials.

BELOW LEFT

This special arrangement of flowers in a number of different shades of pink makes an attractive display in a handsome silver dolphin container. The flowers and berries flow beautifully through the arrangement and the nerine in particular makes a glorious sweep of colour through the centre. The bowl of this container is rather shallow and only holds a small glass container so it needs constant filling. Where the size of the stems in an arrangement permits, the use of a block of Oasis could help overcome this problem.

RIGHT

Wooden boxes can make superb containers for a special flower arrangement, particularly if the inside of the lid is decorative and can be featured. Here, because an antique tea caddy is used, the box is lined with polythene for extra security so no water marks will occur to spoil the box, then a bread tin is placed inside to hold the water. The tin holds a ball of wire netting in the usual way.

The flowers have been arranged in a low flowing way so that the beauty and detail of the box, including the leather cover on the inside of the lid, can be seen clearly.

LEFT	RIGHT
Nerine	*Rosa* 'Baccara'
Dianthus	*Rosa* 'Garnet'
Cynara	*Rosa* 'Mercedes'
Beta	*Rosa canina* and *R.*
Rosa 'Carol'	*gallica* (hips)
Astrantia	*Crataegus oxycantha*
Senecio	*Nerine*
Cineraria	*Dianthus* 'William Sim'
Potentilla	*Fagus*
Euonymus	
Pennisetum	

LEFT
The first Christmas roses from the garden are often very short stemmed and in many cases the blooms have been damaged by the Winter weather conditions, but they make a pleasing Winter arrangement combined with holly, ivy and pine. To prevent frost and pest damage, cover the plants with a cloche as the buds appear and place peat or ashes around the plants.

BELOW
Hyacinths last well and fill the room with fragrance when growing as a pot plant or as a cut flower. These early white ones have been arranged in a flat copper dish with a few stems of 'Paper White' narcissi, hellebores and mixed Winter foliages consisting of pine, ivy trails and berries.

RIGHT
This arrangement in a cherub vase has been made up from washable silk flowers. Silk flowers are easy to arrange and give a fairly natural appearance. It is important to choose the colours carefully and to grade the shapes and sizes just as one would do when arranging fresh flowers.

In this group it is possible to pick out spray carnations, variegated ivy, small roses, eucalyptus, and a form of petunia.

ABOVE
Helleborus niger
Hedera
Pinus

RIGHT
Hyacinthus
Narcissus
  'Paper White'
Helleborus
Pinus
Hedera

ABOVE

Chrysanthemum
  'Verdova'
Pinus
Cornus alba
  atrosanguinea
Rhus cotinus purpureus
Setcretia

ABOVE
Branches covered with lichen are useful in Winter when flowers are scarce and expensive. They make a delightful framework for just a few large blooms and the green-grey colourings go well with pink and mauve chrysanthemums arranged in pewter. Lichen is a fungus which develops on dead or dying branches and will only grow in very wet conditions. It develops on many types of trees in old neglected orchards and deciduous woodlands. When not in use, the branches, which are very brittle, should be stored carefully in a damp atmosphere. If the fungi do become dry, they can usually be brought back into good condition by soaking in a bath of lukewarm water.

Bracket fungi and any other forms of lichen on stone and wood can be used from time to time. They will keep well if stored carefully but will not grow if kept dry.

Lichen on branches is occasionally available in flower shops although you should always keep an eye open for it when travel-ling around the countryside. You should be able to pick up beautifully shaped branches that would probably never come to market because of the difficulty of transporting them.

Another rather pretty decoration which is easily made for the Winter time, when fresh flowers are in short supply, is made with elegant sprays of larch, magnolia or lime branches and if they have some lichen on them so much the better. To give the branches a little highlight, first lightly varnish them, then, with a quick-drying glue, attach very small helichrysum or immortelle flowers to the stem in clusters. This will give the appearance of little blossoms on the branches. Allow them to dry thoroughly and arrange them in a suitable container. The secret is to work very carefully with your glue so the stems do not look messy. I like to see these stems in an oriental-style container, and they can be fixed onto an old pinholder, held firmly with some decorative stones. This is more attractive than many decorations on sale before Christmas.

Driftwood is used mostly as an accessory, although it can be the basis of a complete arrangement. At the Flower School we rarely use it but it is attractive when carefully chosen.

Some florists will sell pieces of driftwood, but they seldom have just the piece you are looking for. If you often use driftwood, keep pieces fixed permanently to bases and then you can add the flowers each time to complete the picture.

Driftwood is found at the side of lakes or on the sea shore where it has been brought up by the tide. Interesting shaped branches are also occasionally found in woodland areas where branches and sometimes trees have died and eventually fallen. It is best to make a collection of pieces from which to choose the necessary shape, as it takes a very sharp eye to select the right piece.

Driftwood can be used in its natural form, which blends in very well with flowers and plant materials, or it can be polished by

sanding it down to a really smooth surface and applying a stain polish or varnish. Some people use it in a bleached form which can be obtained by soaking it in a household bleach for a day or so before drying and polishing.

The choice of materials and the selection of the correct piece of driftwood calls for great artistic ability and I admire some of the work which I have seen, but I do not like to see a lot of wood at the expense of flowers. I was once asked to judge a competition entitled 'Use of wood'. Some of the entries had so much wood that it was more like a forest scene than a flower show!

Polished offcuts of wood make excellent bases for some arrangements, especially those in Autumn colourings or when dried materials have been used.

In this arrangement are two pieces of pine roots washed by the waves at the lakeside over many years. They were fixed in the trough with plasticine and the other materials are arranged in a pinholder and netting.

ABOVE
Narcissus
Garrya eliptica
Hedera

107

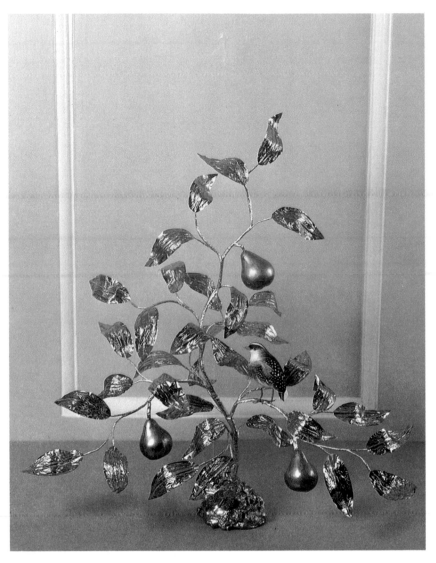

Decorating a Christmas tree

If possible, choose a tree with evenly spaced branches, and prune out any short bushy stems on the main trunk before decorating it. This gives more space to display the decorations and prevents the finished effect from looking heavy. The tree in this photograph was nailed to a silver birch log: a firm base is most important, particularly if there are children around, as a tree that is not securely anchored will topple over easily. If the tree has roots, it can be potted into a large clay flower pot or wooden tub. Place several bricks or stones in the pot with the soil or sand to give added weight and support.

Fairy lights, if used, should be put on first. Space them out evenly over the tree and try to ensure that they do not run in lines or rings around the branches. Fasten the light wires to the branches with short pieces of florist's wire or green string. For this tree a colour scheme of green and gold was chosen to harmonize with the colour scheme in the room. Unless one is decorating a very large tree, it is usually more effective to stick to one or two colours for the trimmings.

The star at the top of this tree was fixed in position after the lights were secured. Gold and green bows and streamers were added to make a strong bold topknot. Large bows of similar ribbon decorate the base and help to hide the light flex where it is not hidden under the carpet. The fairy was then placed in a prominent position where the branches were rather sparse.

To achieve a feeling of weight down the centre of the tree, use some of the bolder decorations close to the main trunk, keeping the lighter and smaller pieces to the outside. Colours should be roughly balanced out over the whole tree, keeping most of the darker and heavier trimmings towards the base. Where baubles or bells are used, they are attached either singly or in clusters, using a ribbon bow to hold them in place. Garlands of tinsel on a Christmas tree often have the effect of dividing it into sections and hiding the other decorations. One of the prettiest ways of using tinsel is to take short lengths and hang baubles or bells from them, and this will give an added sparkle to the overall effect of the tree.

ABOVE This 'partridge in a pear tree' decoration can be made at home quite simply.

RIGHT In common with other types of arrangement, a Christmas tree should be decorated with care and thought.

Partridge in a pear tree

Cut out 35 leaves from a sheet of lurex paper. Cover 35 stem wires with fine strips of green crêpe paper and attach one to the back of each leaf with adhesive tape. Trim off any excess tape with scissors so that none is showing from the front. The leaves can be tooled with a heated tooling iron to give a textured surface. Cover the crêpe paper on the stems with 5 mm ($\frac{1}{4}$ inch) wide strips of gold crinkle paper. Paint three plastic pears with gold paint. The base of the tree is made from plasterer's cement mixed with a little water to a stiff consistency. When dry it is painted with gold paint. The little partridge, bought from a shop, is attached by its wired feet.

Plastic maidenhair fern tree

Take all the individual branchlets off the main stems of two large pieces of plastic maidenhair fern and attach a florist's stem wire to each branchlet. Varnish each fern spray and sprinkle with silver glitter. Make a stem for each of the pine cones with reel wire, varnish them and sprinkle on a mixture of gold and green glitter.

Attach one cone to each of the fern sprays by twisting the finer wire round the heavier one.

Cover the wires with narrow strips of green crêpe paper cut on the bias. Start binding the wires of the branchlets together with fine wire to form the top of the main stem, working down the stem.

Cover the stem with crêpe paper strips, hiding each wire as it is added. Gradually make bigger branches by joining three sprays together. This widens the tree as it nears the base.

Incorporate some extra plain wires to thicken the main stem and give extra support to the increasing weight.

When all the branches have been added, bind the remaining stem firmly with crêpe paper, fastening the end down with glue.

Bend out a few wires at the bottom and make a base with plasterer's cement, mixed to a stiff consistency.

When thoroughly dry, paint the base and shape the branches into a natural tree form.

The more natural you can make the arrangement, the more effective and attractive it will be.

BELOW RIGHT Waterlily with a tinsel candle table decoration.

BELOW Plastic maidenhair fern tree.

Waterlily with tinsel candle

Cut out eight large leaf shapes and five smaller leaf shapes from a double thickness of heavy white net. Keep the shapes in pairs. Cover thirteen thin florist's wires with narrow bias strips of white crêpe paper. Using a clear glue, stick a covered wire down the centre of one leaf, and then stick on the corresponding half. Brush glue round the edge and along the central vein and sprinkle on some fine gold glitter.

Cut some stiff red paper into three feathers, making a series of scissor cuts. With adhesive tape attach both this and the end of a long strip of tinsel to the top of a firm wire. Twist the tinsel round the wire until it is thickly covered. Fill a glass candle-holder with white plasticine and press in first the tinsel candle, then the wires of the eight large leaves, and finally make an inner ring with the five smaller leaves.

Table centre with mistletoe

The sprays of mistletoe are made first. Make
a cardboard template of the leaf pattern
and trace it on the back of some green
crinkle paper which has been folded in half.

When enough leaves have been traced,
cut them out through the double thickness
of paper and place them in pairs with the
green surfaces facing the table. Cover the
back of one leaf with glue and then lay a
thin florist's wire along the leaf. Press the
corresponding half leaf onto the glued piece
and leave it to dry.

When all the leaves are made up, thread
some imitation pearl beads onto wires.
Hold a pair of the leaves around each berry
and bind the three wires together firmly
with thin strips of the green paper. Outline
the sprays of plastic ivy and holly with
clear varnish and sprinkle gold glitter over
them while the varnish is wet.

Press plasticine around the base of the
candle to fill the candleholder. Press the
ends of the leaf sprays firmly into the
plasticine and spread them out to the
desired shape. The bows are made from
wire-edged red ribbon and are inserted on
short wires at the base of the candle to
hide any plasticine which is still showing
around the base.

Robin on a standard holly tree

Mount twelve clusters of artificial plastic
holly onto 30 cm (12 inch) heavy gauge
florist's wires. Cover each wire separately
with 1 cm ($\frac{1}{3}$ inch) wide strips of green
crêpe paper cut on the bias. Attach the
robin's feet to a 30 cm (12 inch) wire and
cover this with crêpe paper.

Holding the holly stems and the robin
wire in a bunch, firmly bind them all
together at a point about 7·5 cm (3 inches)
below the leaves. Cover the remainder of
the long wires with crêpe paper: this forms
the stem of the tree.

Spray a small plastic pot with gold paint.
Put a little plasticine in the bottom to hold
the stem of the tree in position. Then spoon
in enough plasterer's cement mixed with
water to almost fill the pot.
When it has set firmly and dried out
(about 24 hours) paint it with some clear
varnish and sprinkle glitter on top
while the varnish is still wet.

When completely dry, bend the holly
clusters outwards to form a ball shape,
making sure that the robin is at the top.
Attach two bows of ribbon at
the top of the stem where the branches
join and leave the loose ends to hang down
towards the pot.

ABOVE Table centre
with mistletoe (left)
and robin on a
standard holly tree
decoration.

111

Flowers
for children

PAGES 112–3 The maypole for this children's party was made by plaiting ribbon round a pole. A piece of Oasis holds the pole and the flowers (*Dianthus* and *Lathyrus* with *Ruta* foliage).

BELOW *Centaurea* in a small plastic pot covered with nursery-rhyme wrapping paper, and *Viola* and *Adiantum* in an eggshell fixed to a plaster of paris base, with lichen and cones set into it.

Most young children love flowers; I have often watched their faces light up with excitement when they find themselves among flowers, either wild or cultivated ones. This interest should be fostered so they gradually appreciate the beauty of flowers, and they should be encouraged to put them in water and watch them grow.

I can still remember receiving, while in hospital at the age of six or seven, a small pot of grape hyacinths beautifully mossed up. These had been bought so that they could be planted in my own little garden when I got home. What a disappointment it was to find that they were not bulbs at all but that the florist has used cut flowers and just stuck them in damp sand covered with moss!

Containers for children's arrangements can be quite small, and a lot of interesting improvisations can be made. An eggshell could, for example, make a useful container.

Carefully remove the top from a hard-boiled egg without cracking the basal part and remove the contents: a free-range egg will normally have a harder shell. Fill the egg with moist Florapak or damp sand and stand it in a napkin ring or a base made from plaster of paris. Into this can be placed a small posy of wild flowers or some of the small garden flowers such as the baby-rose 'Cecile Brunner', forget-me-nots, fine grasses, gypsophila and flowers from the rock garden.

A jam jar or honey pot can make an excellent flower holder. Fix the pot to a firm circular base of wood or stick a piece of felt to it, then make a covering by glueing pieces of bark and any other interesting material together to hide the container. Cork oak from Portugal is useful as it is very light and easy to work with.

A jar can also be papered with a coarse reeded or Japanese straw paper, but the paper should not get spotted with water because some papers stain easily. An ordinary tin which holds water could be used in this way too, but first check that it has no raw or jagged edges as these can be very dangerous. A coat of paint inside and out will stop it rusting.

There are many kinds of sea shell available today and they can be most attractive filled with simple flowers. Make certain that they will not leak to avoid damaging the furniture. If the shell does not stand well of its own accord, make a plaster of paris base and fix the shell to it. This base can be painted when dry and a piece of felt can be stuck on the underside to finish off the surface and prevent it scratching. Simplicity is important and over-arranging will spoil the effect.

A small basket with a metal lining (a baking tin is ideal) can be most attractive with mixed garden flowers. For a little extra detail, a frill of chintz or gingham in blue or red can be added round the basket, tied on with a drawstring, and the handle covered with the same material.

A log with its base levelled but still retaining the rest of its bark, may be hollowed out in the top to hold a block of Oasis; the base should be painted with pitch and a piece of felt glued to it so that no moisture will filter through to spoil the furniture that it will stand on. Natural wood is ideal for simple flowers of yellow, cream, orange and rust colourings, and a silver birch log looks good with silver-grey foliages and pale shades of pink, mauve and blue.

Although there are no specific rules to follow when arranging flowers for children, the most important thing to bear in mind is that the arrangement should be simple but interesting. The container can play a large part in the charm of the finished arrangement but, as always, the main thing is to choose the plant materials carefully and then let them speak for themselves.

ABOVE A small hamper basket is brightened up with a frill of yellow ribbon and contains *Freesia* and *Hypericum* (in both flower and berry).

ABOVE A miniature basket with wild *Clematis* and side shoots of *Chrysanthemum* 'Crystal'. A shell on its side holds *Zinnia* and *Berberis* in a small piece of Oasis.

A miniature garden, such as the special Easter garden illustrated on the facing page can easily be made by children without going to a lot of expense, as any small wild or garden flowers are suitable. The scheme can be arranged on a fairly wide window ledge, or on a flat board or wooden tray.

First cover the surface with tin foil, waxed paper or fairly strong polythene and on this place little containers to hold the flowers. Aerosol tops or the bases of plastic drinking beakers make ideal pots, or anything else that is about 5 cm (2 inches) deep and the same width across.

For the taller groups of flowers very small pinholders are useful but you can use a small ball of wire netting and put some silver sand in the container. This will weight it down and keep the main stems upright. Silver sand is cleaner than builder's sand.

Collect pieces of moss and lichen to add interest. Bun moss—the thick clumps found growing on roofs and walls—is excellent to place between pieces of stone and bark and will quickly cover the surface around the water pots. Before using bun moss, soak it well to drive out any insects and worms that may be hidden in it. If you buy it from a florist, it may well have been packed in kipper boxes to bring it to market, so will smell very strongly of fish until well soaked and

allowed to drain in the open.

All the flowers to be used should be given the correct treatment to make them last (see Care and handling of cut flowers). Group them into colours and different shapes and decide on a plan as you would for any arrangement; in fact you are doing many small simple arrangements. Fix the height first with some foliage or a slender flower, then set the width with other leaves or flowers and fill in between, getting plenty of variation of length, never putting two flowers the same length next to each other.

Once you have completed the first group, move to the next, working along the line of pots. The number of groups and how they are placed will vary with the size of the base; do not overcrowd them, but allow each group of flowers to show up clearly.

The shorter flowers, such as primroses, double daisies and little violets can be carefully tied into bunches with elastic bands and placed in little clumps towards the front if the garden is to be seen only from there.

Once the garden is set up, moss up around the stone, rock and tree bark, then top up the containers. Do not allow the moss to syphon off the water: this will happen if it is put too close to the pot rim or if the pot is too full of water. The whole area should be sprayed over to help the flowers last and keep the moss green. Top up the pots each day or more often if necessary.

A 'garden' can be used for a table decoration or a low coffee table instead of a vase arrangement but it will only look well on a polished surface. First place a strip of waxed paper down the centre of the table and position the pots at irregular stations, not in one straight line.

The best time of year to do these arrangements is in spring, from the first snowdrops in January right through until about mid-May in the North of England. They can be made up from one flower such as snowdrops, but the wealth of colour and the different shapes of all the small spring flowers really are ideal.

Useful plants for miniature gardens

Allium	*Jasminum*
Anemone	*Muscari*
Chimonanthus	*Myosotis*
Crocus	*Petasites*
Eranthis	*Primula*
Erica	*Prunus spinosa*
Forsythia	*Pulmonaria*
Freesia	*Ranunculus*
Galanthus	*Salix*
Gentiana	*Scilla nutans*
Hedera	*Tulipa*
Helleborus	*Tussilago farfara*
Hyacinthus	*Viburnum*
Iris reticulata	*Viola*

BELOW A miniature garden made in Spring, and containing *Salix*, *Narcissus* 'Silver Chimes', *Allium*, *Forsythia*, *Cheiranthus*, *Laurustinus*, *Anemone*, *Fritillaria meleagris*, *Primula*, *Muscari*, *Hyacinthus*, *Myosotis*.

Special
arrangements

1

2

3

4

Large groups

Do the arrangement in the permanent position as a large arrangement cannot be moved. A bowl is by far the best container to stand on a pedestal as it allows the maximum amount of room for stems and when filled with water is fairly heavy and will sit well on the pedestal. To add extra weight, tie something heavy on the netting at the back of the bowl, or even two blocks of Oasis placed well towards the back. A little extra care when setting up the container will be well repaid in the long run.

If the materials are short in the stem, it will help to work with flower cones set up on square stakes and firmly fixed into the netting. Five or seven is the usual number to use but this will depend on the overall finished size. The stakes can be painted dark green, but if the flowers are well arranged no cones or stakes should show. Proportion between flowers and vase is of the utmost importance and although one cannot lay down rules, I think that arranging the flowers in the following way will help.

⚓ As usual, first fix the background foliage. This should be trimmed and shaped to give a pleasing effect and should be placed at least two-thirds of the way towards the back of the vase, leaning back very slightly. If many flowers are to go into the vase, place the background foliage right at the back, but allow for the curve of the container wall. Stand well back at this stage to see that you have the correct height and change it now if necessary, because once flowers are added it will be impossible to take out the background foliage. It is important to get the correct proportion and only your own taste and experience will guide you here.

⚓ Next, set the width to the arrangement, choosing shapely pieces (trimming to exaggerate a curve will help), anchoring the stems under the netting at the back of the vase. If Oasis is being used, set them firmly into this.

⚓ When the outline is settled, stand well back once again to see the overall picture. Your flowers may go to the outline but should never extend beyond it.

⚓ The flower cones or tubes are the next to go in, the fewer the better. Fill them with water and put a small piece of netting in each.

⚓ At this stage it is a good idea to fix some foliage over the rim of the vase at the front to link the flowers and vase together.

⚓ Next get your main centre flowers in position. They will probably be large blooms, such as lilies. Then place the smaller flowers carefully in the cones, setting them through the group in sweeps of colour and shapes.

Each particular bloom or special leaf should show up well and all the stems should appear to flow from the centre of the vase. A little foliage should go between the stakes of the cones to disguise them.

⚓ Bring the flowers well out over the front to give the group a three-dimensional effect and to avoid the surprised look of flowers appearing to leap out of the vase: there should be no hard rim showing. Some material should be well recessed to give weight and depth to the group, and this will help the balance. Make use of the flower buds and half-open flowers, using the fully open blooms lower down. The balance of the arrangement should be both actual and visual.

⚓ If the group has to look very large and is more than a facing arrangement, place one or two flowers either side of the centre, facing back from the group to give it more of an all round effect.

ABOVE A large green and white group of stripped lime, *Hosta glauca, Alchemilla, Lilium* 'Regale', *Rosa alba maxima* and *R.* 'Iceberg'.

LEFT Four steps to a pedestal arrangement containing *Phormium, Alnus, Prunus lusitanica, Chrysanthemum* 'Ray', *Lilium* 'Destiny', *Alstroemeria, Gladiolus, Dianthus, Rosa* 'Evergold', *Arbutus*.

PAGES 118 9 *Freesia* flowers, buds and side shoots with *Eucalyptus* foliage.

There is a tendency to overcrowd arrangements because of the fear of the mechanics showing, but an extra leaf or a recessed flower may be enough to hide the netting.

When light feathery materials are used, the stems may be twice the length of those on heavy blooms. Dense colours make materials appear heavier so they must be on shorter stems to look right.

Avoid over-arranging, especially with simple garden materials. It is difficult to be logical about matters of taste—choosing the right material and vase is important, but only *you* can decide what these should be, with the setting in mind. Remember that the background is part of the composition and arrange the group where it is to be displayed.

Remember that flowers may well overbalance as they open and cause large arrangements to topple. This reminds me of an occasion when a very happy day could have ended in just such a disaster. Three of us had gone to Sussex to arrange the flowers for a big wedding—the church, the house and the marquee—and it was all to be in stripped lime, lilies and peonies. The church was so small that only a few flowers would be required in each group to make a big display. One of the places chosen for a group was up above the back of the altar in the little side chapel, a very difficult spot to reach. We borrowed a large pair of steps and luckily there was a fair-sized flat area on which to place the large baking tin that we were using as the container. One of the team stood at a distance and gave directions on size and shape, and the second person held the steps while I placed the flowers in the container—quite a precarious operation!

The lime went in easily and a few large leaves 'broke' the hard rim of the tin and linked the flowers and container together. The lilies then went in and lastly the peony buds—not many, but just enough to give a touch of pink. We carefully topped up the vase with water and opened the fanlight in the old glass window behind the altar.

As is always our practice, the next day we visited the church to see that all was well and to top up the vases and cones. To our horror we found that the vase above the altar had fallen, the altar was soaked with water, and the blue dye of the altar frontal had run into the starched white overmantle! The opening peonies had tipped the balance. We learned our lesson and now weight down containers when using heavy flowers that flow well over the container rim.

1

3

2

4

A tied bunch

This is a useful and attractive way of presenting flowers as a gift. The materials should have a good drink before tying. Select a fairly long straight stem for the back of the bunch. Fix the string to this, a little way from the tip of the stem. Tie in one or two more stems, holding the bunch in one hand and positioning the pieces with the other hand. Continue in this way, adding a little at a time, paying particular attention to colours, shapes and length of materials as in all arrangements. The bunch should have fullness at the front. Finish off with a collar of leaves and a neat decorative bow.

Font decorations

When the font is used for a christening, the flowers should always be a special feature. They can be done in various ways. A florist will measure the circumference of the font and make a frame to fit it. This will be covered with bun moss or flower heads and groups of flowers will be wired at three or five stations around the frame. The main group is in the centre, with one or two smaller groups on either side, and the flowers should hang down over the edge of the font in the form of a shower. The colourings will be in white and green, with blue or pink added, or may be in all pastel shades. Allow plenty of flower-free space at the back of the font for the vicar. It is important that the flowers are not so high that they hide the baby from the view of the congregation.

A person not trained in floristry may arrange flowers in a different way but they can still be effective. If there is a good ledge around the font, small containers can be placed on it and these can be linked with trails of ivy to disguise them and link them together. Place little posies of flowers in these small pots and you will have a charming setting for a christening. If there is no large rim on which to stand little containers, make do with the trails of ivy, which can easily be fixed with a waterproof tape; then place a garland around the base of the font with the flowers standing on the floor. This is attractive when seen from a distance but is not so effective during the service, as all the colour is hidden.

Fonts may also be decorated at other times. Never arrange flowers directly in the font, although it may be possible to get a large bowl to fit into it to take an all-round arrangement. Some fonts have a heavy flat wooden cover—if this is turned upside down, a bowl or large vase can stand on it to take the arrangement. A stone-coloured, old-fashioned mixing bowl is ideal.

For Easter, the font can be treated as for a christening; but with the flowers all the way round. Small flowers like primroses, Roman hyacinths, polyanthus and grape hyacinths will be excellent tucked in thick moss.

At Christmas, use little clusters of holly and berries, variegated and plain groups, mistletoe, pine with cones, and one or two small groups of red flowers, all linked together with ivy trails.

At Harvest Festival use trails of hops between the posies of flowers and, again, use berries, fruits and flowers.

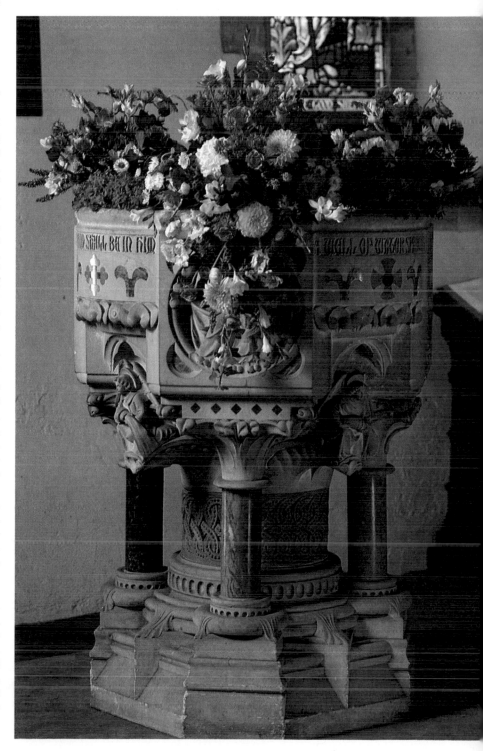

FACING PAGE Four steps to a tied bunch. BELOW A heavy-looking font calls for larger arrangements than usual. Here the mixed flowers are arranged in Oasis bowls and the areas between arrangements are linked with *Ruta* foliage.

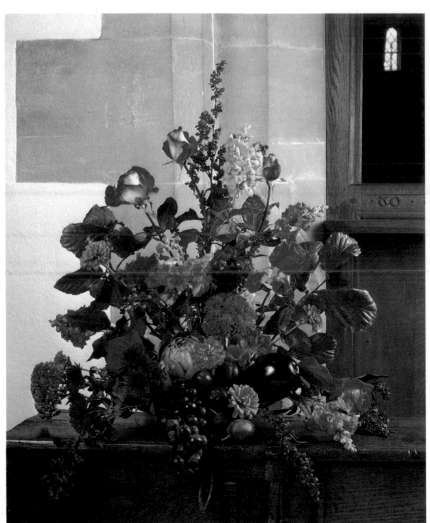

Church arrangements

The general principles of flower arranging also apply to church groups but there are just a few specific points to bear in mind. Always use a strong background foliage to throw the colours of the flowers forward. This is particularly important if blue and mauve colourings are to be used as these are easily lost against stone walls. Although the groups may be large, keep the overall lines of the arrangement quite simple and use a few large flowers in preference to many small ones which will be lost from a distance.

LEFT Harvest colours are traditionally the golden Autumn shades, but here reds, purples, and pinks are based around an artichoke and an aubergine. Sprays of blackberries blend with *Antirrhinum*, *Zinnia*, *Chrysanthemum*, *Hydrangea* and *Sedum*.

BELOW Arrangements at Easter-time often feature *Narcissus*. This church arrangement also includes *Salix*, *Forsythia*, *Berberis japonica*, *Euphorbia*, *Tulipa*, and *Hedera*.

RIGHT BELOW A church window ledge is a good site for an arrangement, as the flowers are in full view yet well out of the way. This harvest festival arrangement shows off a collection of Autumnal fruits and vegetables. The flowers include *Rosa* 'Peace', *Lilium* 'Destiny', *Cotoneaster*, *Azalea*, *Paeonia*, *Dahlia*, *Gladiolus*, *Chrysanthemum*, *Helianthus*.

LEFT An Easter arrangement made up of ten arum lilies and some wild cherry with *Megasea* and *Prunus lusitanica* foliage.

RIGHT This Christmas group of foliages and flowers could be seen at any time of year if it were not for the berries. The height is fixed with the bare wood of *Cornus* and long stems of *Rosmarinus*. *Senecio, Elaeagnus, Eucalyptus, Laurus* and *Ceanothus* are other foliages used, and the centre is a head of *Mahonia bealei*. Berries of *Mahonia gagnepainii, Ilex* and *Hedera* give interest, and the unusual form of *Chrysanthemum* is 'Luyona'.

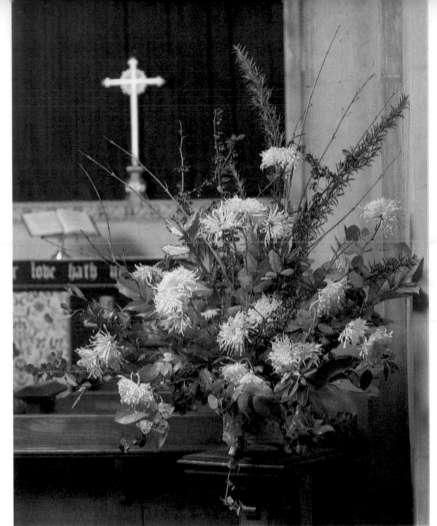

RIGHT Arranging flowers against a colourful or highly decorated background is always a problem. For this Christmas altar group white has been chosen to avoid any clash with the wonderful mosaic behind. The outline of the arrangement is made from *Salix caprea*, just showing silver flower buds, and *Cedrus atlantica glauca*. Variegated holly tends to be rather untidy in growth and these pieces needed some trimming for a good shape. *Fatsia japonica* leaves break the rim of the vase, and the chrysanthemums are 'American Beauty' and 'Bonnie Jean'.

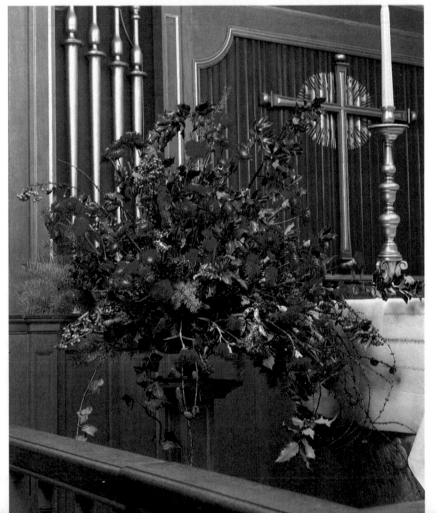

LEFT BELOW This Christmas arrangement in seasonal colourings could either stand on its own at one side of the altar or be one of a pair. The berries are from two varieties of holly, rose hips, *Pyracantha* and tree ivy. The iris seed pods were picked in the Autumn and dried, and a few stems of larch bearing cones trail over the edge of the vase. Flowers are *Dianthus* 'William Sim' and an unknown spray carnation, and *Chrysanthemum*.

Wedding flowers

Wedding flowers create the setting for the wedding ceremony, suggesting a note of welcome to the guests before the arrival of the bride, but it is not a flower festival and the arrangements should not overshadow the beauty of the church itself.

As a general guide, for an average-sized church, six or eight arrangements of flowers would be suitable, and it is better to make prominent groups rather than have flowers dotted around everywhere. Simplicity is the key to success and a few large flowers in the centre of each of the groups will show to good advantage.

Each church will have its own likes and dislikes and it is important to get permission to carry out any decoration within the church. Some churches allow flowers on the altar, others prefer them behind the Holy Table or a group either side of it. Whenever possible, try to use the church's own vases because these are usually in keeping with the rest of the church furnishings.

The flowers at the altar should be simple and there is nothing better than some form of large lily, remembering that many different types of flowers do not show up well from a distance. It is traditional to use white at the altar, and a few well-arranged stems with some clear-cut foliages should be sufficient.

Two very large groups—in fact these are the main flower arrangements at the wedding —should stand on either side of the chancel rail, where they always show to good advantage, as the main part of the wedding service takes place here. These flowers may be all white or in colours which are linked to the bridal party colours. A lot will depend on the type of church and its wall colours; for instance, if decorating an old church which has grey stone walls inside, great care must be taken if using blue flowers, as they will fade into the background colour and be quite lost from a distance, giving the appearance of great gaps in the arrangements. To overcome this, see that a good foil of background green foliage is used to throw the flower colour forward. Some large simple flowers will help at the centre of these groups, for example one of the lilies or large blooms such as peonies, chrysanthemums or hydrangeas.

Another pair of smaller vases will look well standing on either side of the main aisle of the church. These will contain the same type of flowers as those at the chancel rails but should be on a smaller scale and often without the special centre flowers.

When arranging a pair of vases it is important to share the flowers carefully so that each vase has the same materials. It is easy to make one very nice arrangement and then find that there are too few flowers left to complete the other one. It may be that the position calls for identical or symmetrical arrangements, or two arrangements with flowing lines from left to right and right to left.

Whatever the chosen shapes, always set the height of each first, then the width. This can only be done by standing well back after each piece has been placed in position. Once you have the outline, work on the centre, taking care to see that the materials and colours are brought in sweeps rather than blocks of different colours or shapes. When working with really big groups it is important to have long flowing materials. No pleasing flow can be obtained by working with short materials in flower cones, although these aids are ideal for adding to the framework of the arrangement and getting extra amounts of colour or interest where needed.

If the church is to be full of people, consider the use of window ledges: these often prove troublesome because they slope and it is difficult to hold the container in place, but they are ideal positions for flowers, out

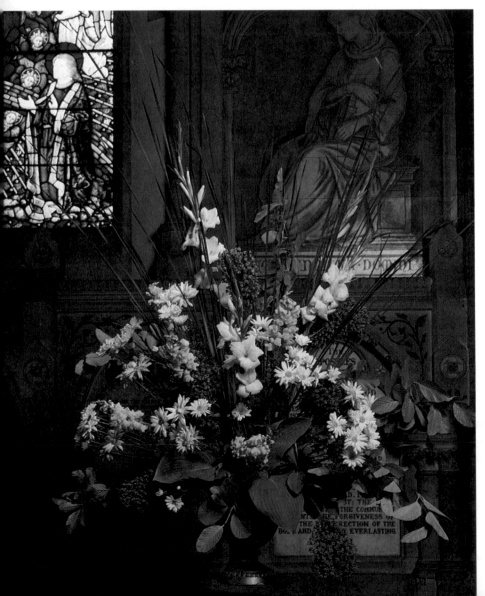

BELOW The altar group at an early Summer wedding in a small country church. The foliages are *Typha, Sorbus aria lutescens, Hosta sieboldiana, Bergenia cordifolia*, and the flowers are *Gladiolus, Euphorbia characias, Chrysanthemum* and *Antirrhinum*.

Bouquets

of the way, yet in full view of everyone. Many churches have overcome the difficulty by providing special platforms for the vases to stand on, and a low container such as a bread-baking tin would be ideal. To help balance it, some stone chippings should be placed in its base. Painted in a neutral stone colour, the container will not show when well arranged. For extra safety, fix a wire from the back of the container to the window frame.

A group at the back of the church is the last thing one sees on leaving after the service. A very nice idea is to have a group of flowers in the entrance porch of the church; a lantern vase hanging inside the porch roof can look very good and may well feature in the photography after the service if a group picture is taken just outside the church.

Flowers for the bride and her bridesmaids are almost as important as the dresses, and the colour and shape of the bouquets form an essential part of the general scheme. This work is carried out by the professional florist and no amateur should attempt it.

In planning a wedding it is well to remember that the procession down the aisle contains an element of pageantry so, although detail is important, a certain uniformity is necessary, and the greater the number of bridesmaids the more clearly this should be emphasized. It is important that the bridesmaids should, irrespective of their individuality, act as one and strive to make the wedding procession as beautiful, flowing and harmonious as possible.

ABOVE An arrangement in the Marquee. The vase, three cherubs holding up a bowl, is ideal to stand on a buffet as it raises the material well above the table. The materials are *Tellima, Eucalyptus, Chrysanthemum, Helleborus, Mahonia bealei, Hosta, Dianthus, Delphinium.*

129

Dried flowers

ABOVE This little picture is made from small pieces of dried materials which one would normally throw out as being too small to use. The pieces have been joined together and then glued to the fabric before mounting and framing.

PAGES 130–1 This arrangement has been done in a small piece of Oasis which is fitted into a shallow shell. The shell rests on a brass twin dolphin base which came from a tray of oddments at a junk shop. The foliage is tips of *Eucalyptus* which have been placed in a solution of glycerine for a short while; all the other materials have been air-dried. The height of the vase is made from *Delphinium* and sprays of *Erica*. The other flowers are *Statice sinuata* and *Acroclinium*.

Towards the end of the year, when little is available from the garden, I like to make use of dried materials to help with flower decorations although, to my mind, nothing can take the place of a few fresh flowers.

Today there are many very real-looking plastic and other artificial flowers for special work such as in the theatre, but they cannot match real dried ones, which retain some of their original life and movement. With many dried flowers coming from abroad there is a wealth of material to use but the natural and bleached colourings are the most effective.

I prefer to use dried flowers in the late Autumn and Winter and store them for the Spring and Summer. They will keep over the years but they become brittle as they get older. It is important to keep them clean and free from dust, and when not in use, stored in boxes between sheets of tissue paper in a dry place. They will soon go mouldy if they become damp. You can store them in large plastic bags to which a little drying agent, such as silica gel, has been added, but keep natural coloured stems in the dark to prevent them fading. Remember also to keep an eye on them, because they are attractive to mice.

The range of materials which can be dried is vast and gives scope for many colour schemes. Trees and shrubs, roses, herbaceous plants, ferns and grasses all respond to drying. Dried materials can be divided into two main groups: flowers in bright colours which are harvested from the garden or bought in the early Autumn, and foliages and seed heads which tend to be more sombre in their brown-green colourings; both are useful. All

these materials can be used during the summer as fresh flowers and foliages so, if you have room to grow them in the garden, they serve a dual purpose.

It is most important to harvest at the correct time, and only perfect materials should be used if they are to dry properly and keep their character, although they always lose a little of their colour during the drying process. It is a waste of time to harvest and dry partially damaged or weathered materials because any marked tissue will tend to show up more distinctly as the drying takes place. Drying and preserving should be done straight after picking.

The art of drying and preserving is very skilled and makes a fascinating hobby, though it can be time-consuming and take up rather a lot of room if done in a big way. Some plant materials will dry well if hung upside down, or if covered with silica gel or borax and packed in boxes.

Many types of foliage such as beech, eucalyptus, hornbeam, stripped lime and oak, to name a few, can be preserved with a solution of glycerine and water in equal parts. Some people say that for the soft-leaved foliages one part glycerine to two parts water is quite sufficient, but the stronger or tougher the leaves, the stronger the solution needed. At the Constance Spry Flower School we always dry all foliages in a mixture of equal parts.

Dissolve the glycerine in near-boiling water. Stand the stems, not too many at a time, in a fairly deep container while the solution is still warm. There should be at least 15 cm (6 inches) of liquid covering the base of the stem. Glycerine is quite expensive, so if you propose to use a lot of it, it would be cheaper to buy the commercial type from a chemist. A glycerine-based anti-freeze can be used but some contain a dye which may discolour your material.

Carefully select well-shaped branches as it is pointless to treat pieces that will not be of use afterwards. Remove any damaged and unwanted shoots (these small pieces, if preserved in the same way, can be used to fill in an arrangement) and then hammer the base of the stem. If the bark is very thick, peel some off to show the white wood below (this will help it take up the glycerine solution). Be sure that the foliage is mature but not too advanced before commencing treatment, otherwise some of the leaves may fall before the glycerine is absorbed. Once Autumn colours have started to appear on the leaf, natural chemical changes have taken place and the supply of moisture to that leaf has been cut off so the glycerine will never reach it.

Allow the stems to stand in the solution in a cool, dark place until the foliage shows a change in colour. The time the process takes will vary with the different foliages and, to a certain extent, the temperature in which you are working. It usually takes a few days, but hard woody materials like laurel and rhododendron may take weeks. It is important to take them out when the undersides of the leaves appear slightly oily. Never leave them longer because once this occurs the surface will be slightly sticky and pick up dust very quickly. The stems can now be stored in a large container in a cool, dry, airy place.

Some leaves can be totally immersed but you need a shallow bath in which to float the individual leaves. As soon as they start to change colour, lift them from the solution, and wash and dry them quickly on blotting paper in a warm place.

Many flowers are dried as heads and are then mounted on false stems made of wire or pieces of straw. The wiring of the flowers may be done before drying because a dry stem is often difficult to wire.

Arranging dried materials calls for exactly the same approach as any other flower arrangement, except that one difficulty is resolved; namely, there is no worry about getting a difficult stem to reach the water! All stems should flow nicely from a central point in the container. Shape, balance and proportion are still important but, because of their visual lightness, dried flowers may often be arranged with slightly taller stems than when using fresh flowers and still look correct. The tracery of lime branches, for example, looks wrong if cut down to use in a low dried arrangement.

Choose your materials as you would fresh flowers, to suit the décor of the room, and try to introduce shades that match a colour already predominant. The container is important, and wood or basket work suit dried materials. Metal is also useful, particularly brass and copper for green, brown and bronze colourings. Pewter looks good with mauve-pink and silver-green shades. China and pottery also offer plenty of scope but should normally be in the rather heavy designs rather than delicately shaped fine china. Silver and cut glass are not in keeping with dried materials.

Ordinary wire netting will be perfectly satisfactory to use to hold the stems in position but because many dried stems will be much thinner, having shrunk during drying out, you may find a closer tangle of netting will help you. Let the netting lie along the base of the vase to steady any stems which may move about.

Dry Oasis and Styrofoam (this can only be used dry) are excellent for holding dry materials, but in both cases they must be firmly held in the container before commencing the arrangement. There is a special Oasis pinholder which can be fixed to the base of the Oasis block to weight it when dry. Ordinary pinholders are not much use with dried materials. I like to use a little wire netting with the Oasis because I find it helps to hold the stems more firmly, and a piece of netting can be bent to hold a difficult stem. Dry sand and fine gravel can be used as a last resort; they have the advantage of being heavy, but they tend to be rather messy and it is difficult to get some of the fine stems into them.

ABOVE LEFT This dried arrangement is done in a block of Oasis standing in a wooden cigar box. In the centre are lotus seed heads. The small reed mace, sprayed with hair lacquer to preserve it, sets the height, and the outline foliage is glycerined beech. The large single leaves at the centre are from *Magnolia grandiflora*. Other materials are eucalyptus seed pods, black water grass, wheat, iris seed pods, *Physalis franchetii* and *Helichrysum*. Some of the materials have been dyed or made up artificially.

Materials for drying

Acanthus mollis (Bear's Breeches)
The flowers of this plant can be used in both fresh and dried groups and are interesting in shape and colour. They dry very easily when hung upside down in a dark airy position, or they can be placed in large polythene bags with silica gel for quick drying.

Achillea
These flat heads of yellow flowers are well worth growing for cutting fresh and they dry well. Remove all leaves before treating the stems. They can be hung upside down or laid in flat boxes and dusted in borax. Keep well sealed until fully dried.

Acroclinium (sometimes known as *Helipterum*)
These are fairly small daisy-type flowers and come in pink and white colourings. They are useful in both the fresh and dried form.

Allium
All the onion family are worth drying and range from quite small seed heads to those of considerable size. They dry readily when hung in airy conditions. One disadvantage is that they tend to retain a slight onion smell.

Amaranthus caudatus (Love-lies-bleeding)
This is an excellent plant with long red tassels, and its green form, *A. caudatus* 'Viridis', is sold fresh in some flower shops. It should have its leaves removed and be hung upside down to allow the long tassels to dry. It will fade a little but is very useful in tall dried groups and looks well arranged against a background of a darker foliage.

Atriplex hortensis rubra
This has dark red leaves and a flower head closely resembling spinach. Remove all leaves and hang it upside down. When dried, it has interesting arched branches of pendant seeds. It can be a nuisance in the garden because it readily seeds everywhere.

Helichrysum (Straw Flower)
This is a double daisy flower in shades of white, ivory, lemon, pink, maroon, gold and brown. It is grown from seed each year and requires a well-drained and sunny situation to develop well. The stems need careful staking and support to remain straight. They should be cut when fully developed, have the basal leaves removed, be tied in bunches, and hung upside down to dry in an airy, shaded place. For perfect flowers, pick each one just as it starts to open and dry it in a box containing a drying agent, such as silica gel.

Hydrangea
Some varieties are much better than others for drying. The colours range from white, green, deep pink and red to pale and deep blue. The flowers must be cut when they have lost their first softness and are becoming slightly papery and crisp to the touch. They can be dried hung upside down in an airy place or placed in a vase of water, allowing the water to be absorbed gradually, or in a solution of glycerine and water.

Limonium latifolium (Sea Lavender)
Sometimes called perennial statice. It is not unlike gypsophila in habit and has a tiny blue flower which dries well. It is best dried standing upright in a plastic bucket, away from bright light, allowing plenty of air and space between the stems.

Lunaria biennis (Honesty)
Although normally grown for the silvery, moon-shaped membranes between the seed pods, the whole seed pods of this plant can be used, and their grey-green colour suits some arrangements better than the natural silver of the central membrane. The stems must be dried as soon as they are fully developed; if left too long the seed stains the silver membranes. When the outer seed cases are dry they will easily peel off. They are now sold dyed in many colours but are better used in their natural colour.

Molucella laevis (Bells of Ireland)
This does well in some seasons but is not always successful. It is now often sold as a cut flower, imported from Kenya and South America in its green form. The tall slender square stems look well in large arrangements and it has beautiful papery green cup-shaped calyxes. It takes glycerine well and can also be bleached by drying in heated conditions. All foliage should be removed carefully before drying.

Physalis (Chinese Lantern)
The interest in this member of the potato family lies not in its flowers but in the pretty orange/scarlet seed heads which remain at the end of the season and hang like lanterns down the stem. One form, *P. edulis*, is grown for its edible fruit. Dry it by hanging it up, having first bunched it into a small number of stems. Remove the leaves as they dry and, when the lanterns are completely dry, lay in a box with a little silica gel.

Statice sinuata
This is sold in August and September as a fresh flower and dried for use in the Winter months. It comes in white, yellow, mauve and pink, and is often available as a mixed bunch. It is very long lasting and needs

thinning carefully to get a good shape before arranging. Another statice which can be dried is *S. suworowii* and this has long square stems of lilac pink flower sprays.

Ferns and bracken are best dried between newspaper just as they are taking up colour in the autumn. Leave them under a carpet to keep them flat and they should dry well in a few weeks. Ornamental grasses have many shapes and sizes and are useful either on their own or arranged with mixed flowers. There are many other plants that can be dried and you should experiment with other annuals and materials from the flower border. Seed heads are very useful and should be cut from the plant when nearly dry but not weathered. A walk along a country lane can provide many more items, but protected plants must not be gathered (see page 14).

BELOW All the materials in this cupid vase come from the garden and have been dried naturally, with the exception of the box (*Buxus*) which has been bleached and glycerined.

A-Z

Abutilon
P. Summer.
This plant is grown essentially for its foliage, but the small flowers can be used. Flowers: bell shape, orange with red veins, not long lasting. Foliage: variegated due to a virus. *A. megapotamicum* E.S. (greenhouse): flowers have red caps with yellow petals on small graceful arching sprays.
● Hot water for both foliage stems and flower sprays.

Acacia
Mimosa. E.T. and S. * From February.
Flowers: yellow, very short lived in their fluffy state. Foliage: *A. dealbata* has many leaflets forming compound leaves giving it a fluffy appearance; *A. longifolia* has a long linear leaf.
● Use on its own, not mixed with other flowers. Keep sealed up in the cool until needed. It is best in a moist atmosphere.

Acanthus mollis
Bear's Breeches. P. Summer.
Flowers: white and purple, tubular on long spikes; dry well. Foliage: thistle-like.
● Young material will not last long so foliage must be fully developed before it is cut and then given a long drink before arranging. Flower stems are hollow and may benefit from filling with water and plugging.

Acer
Maple. D.T. and S. * common form only. May–Autumn.
The common field maple is lovely when just opening in Spring. Japanese maples are very decorative small shrubs. Maples have lovely Autumn colourings and attractive bark.
● Hammer woody stems and soak for a few hours in water. Revive when necessary by placing tips in boiling water. Some of the fine-leaved varieties may have difficulty taking up water.

Achillea
Yarrow. P. * Early Summer–Autumn.
A. filipendulina: flowers are various shades of yellow, sometimes sold dried. *A. millefolium* 'Cerise Queen': flowers are pink, long lasting, and strong smelling. *A. ptarmica* 'The Pearl': flowers are white and their round pompom shape is quite different from other yarrows.
● Remove lower foliage as it smells in water. Dry by hanging upside down or lay the flower heads dusted in borax in a box.

Acidanthera
Corm. * September–November.
Flowers: white with purple spot at base of flower; fragrant and long lasting.

Aconitum
Monkshood. P. Summer.
Flowers: purple-coloured flower spike, useful for mixed Summer arrangements; lasts well. Similar to some delphiniums but has a much smaller flower spike. The roots of this plant are poisonous. Dry the seed head by hanging upside down.

Adiantum
Maidenhair Fern. P. * cut and as a pot plant. Most of the year.
Foliage: useful for bouquets and it goes particularly well with sweet peas in arrangements. Most attractive when arranged on its own giving a cool effect.
● Burn cut tips to seal stem. Float in a bath of water for a good drink.

Agapanthus
African Lily. P. * July–September.
Flowers: blue or white on long leafless stems, useful for large groups but not long lasting. The many small flowers which make up the round heads are wired singly by florists in bouquets. Seed-bearing heads can be dried for Autumn.
● A long drink is necessary before they are arranged.

Agrostemma
syn. *Lychnis* (q.v.)

Alchemilla mollis
Lady's Mantle. P. * June–August. One of the most useful plants, this mixes well with many flowers. Flowers: sharp green colour.
● Remove basal leaves and give a good drink before arranging

Allium
Lily family, related to onions. Bulb. * May–August.
Flowers: yellow (*A. moly*), white (*A. triquetrum*), red and green (*A. siculum*), bright lilac (*A. giganteum*); sizes vary; many good as dried seed heads.

Alnus
Alder. D.T. * February and March.
Use when in flower or leaf; branches are elegantly shaped and carry catkins and cones at the same time. The catkins make a lot of pollen dust when fully out.
● Cut alder in December and bring it into the warm to force it.

Alstroemeria
Peruvian Lily. P. * Nearly all year round from glasshouse crops, outdoor flowering June–August.
Flowers: cream and yellow, red, pink and mauve, orange and yellow, white, brown; long slender stems; last well in water. Foliage: rather untidy and is easily damaged when packed for market. Stems are easily cut down to be used in small arrangements. It is a very useful plant.
● Remove basal leaves and stand in deep water for a few hours to really charge the stems with moisture.

Althaea rosea
Hollyhock. P. July.
Flowers: pastel cream, pink, white or yellow; old fashioned double and single form. Suitable for a large group or a Dutch group; last well.
● Hollow stems.

Amaranthus caudatus
Love-lies-bleeding. A. * August–October.
Flowers: green or red, can be dried; best in tall groups where hanging panicle can show to good advantage.
● Remove most of the leaves before placing in deep water. Stems may be woody some seasons and need splitting.

Amaryllis belladonna
Belladonna Lily. Bulb. * August–October.
Flowers: pink flower spike; long lasting; leafless stem.
● Cut stems at an angle and allow a long drink.

Amelanchier
D.S. Spring and Autumn.
White-flowered shrub in April. Good Autumn colour.
● Remove some of the foliage to allow full benefit from flowers. Woody stem.

Anchusa
P. Summer.
Flowers: blue, stems like large forget-me-nots up to 1 metre (3 feet) tall; long lasting.
● Remove many of the basal leaves. This plant wilts easily.

Andromeda floribunda
syn. *Pieris floribunda* (q.v.)

Anemone
Tuber. * October–June.
Flowers: colourful and

● As for gladioli

long lasting. Double and single forms, some named varieties such as 'The Bride' (white) and September Charm' are good.
● Give a long drink up to their necks in water before arranging. Does not last well in Oasis.

Anemone pulsatilla
syn. *Pulsatilla vulgaris* (q.v.)

Angelica
P. * June onwards. Useful for seed heads in late Summer but not long lasting as flowers. Up to 2 metres (6 feet) tall.
● Put in water straight after cutting, place a cane in hollow stem and plug.

Anthemis
P. July–August. Flowers: yellow daisy, long lasting. Foliage: aromatic, fernlike.

Anthurium
Flamingo Flower. P. * All year round glasshouse flower. Flowers: white, cream, coral or scarlet. Useful for modern arrangements and last well.
● Warm water if limp.

Antirrhinum
Snapdragon. A. * March–June, late Autumn. Flowers: long single flower stems, red, pink, white, orange, yellow; long lasting, useful for big arrangements. Some very good hybrid forms.
● Give a deep long drink before arranging and remove much of the lower foliage. The early crops from glasshouses have rather fragile stems.

Aquilegia
Columbine. P. * Early Summer. Flowers: cottage garden type: pretty pastel shades which

arrange well in pewter, copper and silver; last well, buds keep opening. Foliage: attractive Autumn colours.

Aralia elata
E.S. Autumn–Winter. Foliage: individual ivy-type leaves, good for centre of flower group.
● Place leaf tips in boiling water then immerse stems in cold water for a good long drink.

Arbutus
Strawberry Tree. E.T. * Sometimes October–December. Flowers: strawberry-like fruits at the same time as small white bell-shaped flowers (October–December); unusual in arrangements. Foliage: thin out leaves to let fruits show up well.

Arctotis
A. Late Summer. Flowers: daisy flowers, close up at night; many hybrid colour forms, quite long lasting.

Arisarum proboscideum
Mouse Plant. P. March–May. Flowers: mouse-like in appearance—stalk 7–15 cm (3–6 inches) long, spathe greyish white and inflated with long curved tail up to 12 cm (5 inches); interesting flower for children. Foliage: small arum-shaped leaves.

Armeria
Thrift. P. June–August. Flowers: white, pink or lilac; useful in small arrangements.

Artemisia
A. abrotanum (Southernwood), *A. absinthium* (Wormwood). P. Late Spring–Summer.

Foliage: aromatic silver-grey.
● Place tips in boiling water, then give a long drink before arranging.

Arum italicum pictum
P. Autumn, Winter and Spring. Foliage: beautifully veined and arrow-shaped in varying sizes: red berries last well and appear after the flowers in late summer.
● Soak thoroughly before use.

Arundinaria
Bamboo. P. * dried. All year round. Best used as a dry material, does not take water well.
● Press under carpet to keep from curling.

Asparagus
P. * (outdoor and greenhouse grown). All year round. *A. officinalis*: July and August. After taking the edible tops of young sprouts, cut as foliage. *A. plumosus* (Asparagus Fern): formerly used in large quantities as the background to flowers in wedding bouquets. *A. sprengeri*: often grown in hanging baskets, can be cut but watch for spiteful thorns. *A. asparagoides* (Smilax): available most of the year, used for garlanding.

Aspidistra
Houseplant. * All year. Foliage: dark green and variegated forms; use as single leaves in mixed greens; bleached leaves are used with dried materials.
● Submerge in water to get a good drink before arranging.

Asplenium
P. Fern. * *A. bulbiferum*. All year

round. This is the fern that produces little plantlets on the fronds which root readily. Cut and use the fronds with mixed greens.
● Submerge in water for a long drink.

Aster
Michaelmas Daisy. P. * July–October. Flowers: daisy-type; blue, white, pink or red; many are subject to mildew and wilt; useful for large mixed autumn groups.
● Stems of some are woody so hammer well before giving a long drink.

Astilbe
False Goat's Beard. P. * June–August as a pot plant. Flowers: pink and white colours.
● Hammer stems and place tips in hot water. Foliage curls up very quickly if it becomes at all dry.

Astrantia
P. June and July. Flowers: artificial looking, silvery pink-green with deeper pink centre. Foliage: does not last well in water if left on long stems. Variegated foliage form of *A. minor* is excellent.
● Plunge into water straight after cutting. Dry by hanging upside down.

Atriplex
Orach, a form of spinach. A. July–August. Flowers: crimson colouring. Seeds very readily; can be dried.
● Remove basal leaves and give a long drink; stems may be woody if it is grown under dry conditions so hammer well if necessary.

Aucuba
Spotted Laurel. E.S. March–April (berries), April–May (flowers).

* as a growing plant. Foliage: useful for mixed greens or centre of a large group; lasts well.

Auricula
P. April–July. Flowers: old-fashioned type, allied to polyanthus; useful for small arrangements; longer lasting than polyanthus. Foliage cannot be used.

Azalea
E. and D.S. (Correctly known as Rhododendron). * Cut stems April–June and late Autumn and Winter as pot plants. Flowers: superb range of colours, shape and size; show off well in copper and pewter containers, long lasting.
● Woody stems. Pot plants must always be kept moist.

Begonia
P. * as a pot plant. Most of the year. A very large group of plants—can be divided into flowering and foliage plants. The 'Rex' group are the main foliage ones. Some of the species are very pretty and last well when cut. The large-flowered varieties do not last when cut.
● Submerge foliage before use.

Berberis
Barberry. E. and D.S. * Late Winter–June. Flowers and berries are useful. Foliage: attractive Autumn colour and a variety of leaf shapes. Best varieties are *B. darwinii*, *B. gagnepainii*, *B. thunbergii atropurpurea*, *B. wilsonae*.
● Put in hot water after hammering stems.
Spines can be poisonous.

Bergenia
syn. *Megasea*, Giant Saxifrage, Elephant's Ears. All year round (foliage), Spring and Summer (flowers). Flowers: *B. cordifolia* are pink in March, *B. crassifolia* are deep red in May, June. Foliage: flat leathery rounded leaves in a variety of shapes and colours. Only use mature leaves.
● Float leaves before use if soft to allow them to absorb plenty of moisture.

Betula
Birch. T. Spring and Summer.
Branches: light tracery, some catkins in early Spring. Silver grey bole.
● Hammer base of stem.

Bocconia
syn. *Macleaya* (q.v.)

Briza gracilis
Quaking Grass. A. * sometimes. Late Summer.
To dry: hang up young grass in Autumn in small bunches in an airy room.

Brodiaea uniflora
Bulb. * April–May. Flowers: pale lilac and star-shaped on leafless stems; long lasting.

Buddleia
Semi-E.S. May–August.
B. davidii (July–August) is common; *B. globosa* (May–June) is unusual with bright yellow fragrant flower balls.
● Remove most of the foliage and hammer the stems.

Buxus
Box. E.S. * common form only. Nearly all year.
Foliage: variegated small-leaved varieties with white edge to leaf are the most interesting; long

lasting and good for mixed greens.
B. sempervirens argentea or *B. aurea maculata* are recommended.
● Hammer woody stems.

Caladium
Houseplant. * All year round.
Foliage: large arrow-shaped leaves—reds, pinks, cream and greens; place the whole pot plant in the centre of a large arrangement.
● Will not stand draughts or cold conditions.

Calendula
Pot Marigold. A. * March–October. July–October in the garden.
Flowers: colourful, particularly the cream and yellow and pale orange shades; not long-lasting and flowers always tend to face upwards.
● Long drink before arranging.

Calla aethiopica
syn. *Zantedeschia aethiopica* (q.v.)

Callistemon
Bottle Brush. E.S. June–August.
Flowers: red, resemble a bottle brush.
● Hard woody stems. Best to cut into the wood just below the flower and not the really old wood.

Callistephus
China Aster. A. * August–October.
Flowers: various forms from small buttons to large shaggy flowers; pink, red, mauve, blue and white; last well.
● Remove all foliage from base of stem to stop unpleasant smell in water; some stems may be quite woody.

Calluna vulgaris
syn. *Erica vulgaris* (q.v.)

Camellia japonica
E.S. * Foliage mainly in Autumn and Winter. Flowers in Spring.
Flowers: on short stems and very fragile. Foliage: often shows yellowing on leaves which is very attractive.
● Woody stems; never cut when young growth is soft.

Campanula
Bellflower. A.B. and P. * July and August.
Flowers: long lasting bell shapes in blue, mauve, white and pink; some stems may be woody. *C. medium* 'Calycanthema' (Canterbury Bell) is the old fashioned cup and saucer variety. It is a biennial. *C. persicifolia* is the usual market variety. It is a perennial.

Canna
Indian Shot Plant. P. Summer.
Flowers: red and yellow, not always successful in England. Foliage: some red-coloured, good for large groups, rather similar to Dieffenbachia in habit but self-coloured and variegated.
● Place in deep water straight after cutting.

Carpinus betulus
Hornbeam. D.T. Spring and Summer.
Foliage: good-shaped branches for backing a large group; takes glycerine well for Winter use.
● Hammer stems.

Caryopteris clandonensis
D.S. August–September.
Flowers: blue; last quite well.

Cassinia fulvida
E.S. All year round (foliage) July (flowers).
Foliage: rather like Veronica; yellow-

green, variety of shapes; lasts well.
Flowers: small white heads.

Catananche
Cupid's Dart. A.P. * Summer.
Flowers: blue and white, look rather artificial; useful for mixed small arrangements; good for drying.

Ceanothus
E. and D.S. May–July.
Flowers: blues, last well in water. *C.* 'Gloire de Versailles' is a good variety.
● Woody stems.

Centaurea
Cornflower. A.B. and P. * A. only Summer.
Flowers: perennial form has blue or white flowers, annual form has deep and pale blues, white and wine-red flowers. Foliage: silver-green. *C. montana* is a good perennial form. *C. moschata* (Sweet Sultan) is an annual with white, yellow and purple flowers.

Centranthus
see *Kentranthus*.

Cephalaria tatarica
syn. *Scabiosa elata* (q.v.)

Chaenomeles lagenaria
Quince, Japonica. D.S. Early Spring.
Flowers: red, pink and white; blossom in clusters just when foliage breaks; fruits in Autumn.
● Remove leaves from base of stem.

Cheiranthus
Wallflower. P. (treated as B.) * April and May.
Flowers: sweet-smelling yellow, red, bronze. Not long lasting.
● Hammer stems and remove foliage from near water or it will smell.

Chimonanthus fragrans
Wintersweet. D.S. November–March.
Flowers: pale yellow on leafless branches; fragrant; ideal for specimen vase. Useful Winter shrub.
● Very woody stems need splitting.

Chionodoxa luciliae
Bulb. * sometimes. Early Spring.
Flowers: pretty blue, ideal for moss gardens with snowdrops and primroses.
● Cut stems without any trace of white at base.

Choisya ternata
Mexican Orange Blossom. E.S. * Autumn and Spring.
Foliage: useful all year round.
Flowers: fragrant white.

Chrysanthemum
A. and P. * All year round.
Flowers: single and double compound heads or single blooms; many colours and varieties. Very long lasting and useful. Some people prefer them as an Autumn/Winter flower.
● Hammer stems and give a long drink.

Cineraria maritima
syn. *Senecio cineraria* P. Spring and Summer.
Foliage: silver-grey, good for small arrangements.
Flowers: very insignificant.
● Stems sometimes do not take up water, use young shoots only and hammer well.

Clarkia
A. * Summer.
Flowers: single or double form in mauves, pinks, whites; very useful for cutting. *C. elegans* is the one most commonly grown.

● Soft stem treatment, and remove unnecessary foliage.

Clematis
P. Spring and Summer. Flowers: not long lasting in water but can be very striking in large groups or as a table centre. *C. armandii*: white, April and May; *C. cirrhosa*: cream, January and March; *C. montana*: white and pink, May and June; *C. jackmanii*: large-flowered, mauve, pink, purple, July–October.
● Boiling water for flower stems.

Clivia
Bulb. * Spring and Summer. Flowers: reddish-yellow colour; some cream forms in seedlings. Foliage: evergreen. Often sold in shops as one leaf and one flower stem together.

Cobaea
Cup and Saucer Plant. A. * Pot plants May–June, garden flowers July–October. Requires sun and a wall to grow up. Flowers: trumpet-shaped in violet and cream and green. Can be used when the tubular corolla has dropped and the calyx remains attached to the stem.
● Cut short flower stems and place in water straight away.

Colchicum
Erroneously known as Autumn Crocus. Bulb. Autumn. Flowers: pinkish, particularly pretty in double form; not long lasting.
● Put in water straight after cutting.

Coleus
Nettle family. P. * May–June. Foliage: very

decorative, loses brilliant colouring in Winter.
● Foliage very soft and must go into water immediately after cutting. Single leaves do not last—the whole shoot must be used.

Colutea arborescens
Bladder Senna. D.S. Late Summer. Flowers: yellow-brown pea-shaped flowers followed by bladder-like inflated pods in September.
● Woody stems.

Convallaria majalis
Lily-of-the-Valley. P. * Forced lily-of-the-valley is available all year round. Garden flowers in May–July. Flowers: mostly white, pink form is less popular and seldom seen. Foliage: garden valley has very much darker foliage than the forced valley.
● Place stems in water straight after cutting; use warm water if they are limp and it may help to crush the tips.

Coreopsis
P. * Summer. Flowers: yellow daisy-type, light and delicate; look well arranged with grasses and seed heads.

Cornus
Dogwood. D.S. Winter, Early Spring. *C. mas* (Cornelian Cherry): early flowering—February, March. *C. alba* and *C. stolonifera* have good red-coloured branches in Winter. Wild Dogwood is also a useful flowering shrub.

Cortaderia argentea
Pampas Grass. P. * Autumn. Sharp-pointed reed-like foliage. Useful for large groups in Autumn, such as Harvest Festival and

for dried arrangements. Cut when young and hang upside down for drying. Only grow it if plenty of space is available as it is untidy since dead foliage accumulates around base of clump.

Corylopsis pauciflora
D.S. * Spring. Delicate soft yellow catkins in Spring followed by attractive foliage.
● Woody stem.

Corylus avellana
Hazel. D.T. Autumn–Spring. Cobnuts in Autumn; catkins in Winter and early Spring. Useful dainty foliage. *C. avellana* 'Contorta' has attractive twisted branches.
● Woody stem treatment.

Cosmos bipinnatus
A. * occasionally. Late Summer. Flowers: daisy-type, useful for cutting; mostly pinks, purples and whites; last well. Foliage very light and delicate.

Cotoneaster
D. and E.S. Autumn, Spring. Flowers: late Spring, but more noted for its Autumn berries—red, scarlet, and some yellow and black. Foliage: useful for cutting.

Crataegus
Hawthorn, May. D.S. Autumn and Spring. Good for Spring flowers and Autumn fruiting. Wild variety has a range of berry colours. Some people will not allow it in the house when in flower.

Crinum
Bulb. * occasionally. September and October. Flowers: lily-type; thick fleshy stems.

Grows untidily. Because of its heavy flowers it is only good for large vases.

Crocosmia
Garden Montbretia. Corm. * August–late Summer. Superior form of Montbretia. Flowers: yellow-brown to orange, good lasting qualities. Foliage can be used without flowers—very similar to Iris but smaller.

Crocus
Bulb. * as a pot plant. Spring. Not often used for arrangements because flowers last a very short time when cut; best used in a planted garden on a plate.

Cucurbita
Gourds. A. Late Summer. Fruits: decorative and non-edible; good in mixed fruit groups; should last throughout the Winter.
● Harvest just before the frost and allow to ripen gently in a dry airy place; handle with great care as they can be easily bruised and will then rot; can be varnished but are better natural.

Cyclamen
Corm. * as a pot plant. Autumn and Spring. Flowers: last well when picked. Foliage: excellent in small arrangements and bouquets, some varieties have attractive markings. Never throw a plant away which has finished flowering as the leaves can be used with other flowers.
● Cut the stems once they have been pulled from the corm and place them in warm water for a few hours.

Cynara scolymus
Artichoke, Cardoon. P. * sometimes. Late

Spring and Autumn. Foliage: superb silver-grey large pinnatifid fleshy leaves. Flowers: thistle-like when open, can be dried in Autumn; very attractive when in bud and often used in this stage.
● Place in water straight after cutting; if soft, submerge for a few hours.

Cyperus
Umbrella Plant. P. * as a pot plant. Most of the year. Rush-like grass; interesting shapes to add to a special mixed green arrangement.

Cytisus
Broom. E. and D.S. * April–July. *C. albus*: white. *C. battandieri*: silver foliage, bright yellow flowers May–June. *C. praecox*: creamy-yellow. *C. scoparius* (Scots Broom): many named varieties. Not easy to use as it quickly looks untidy. In modern arrangements some forms of broom are sold in a dry bleached form.
● Woody stems, hot water if soft.

Dahlia
Tuber. * July to first frosts. Flowers: wide colour range, the best for cutting are the small decorative, cacti and pompom types; dahlias are easily bruised.
● Burn cut tips in a flame; hollow stems need filling with warm water.

Daphne
E. and D.S. Spring. Very good scent in Spring; plants die out after a number of years. Good varieties are *D. cneorum* (E.), *D. laureola* (E.), *D. mezereum* (D.), *D. pontica* (D.).

Datura suaveolens
Angel's Trumpet. E.S.
(glasshouse) Summer.
D. stramonium (Thorn
Apple) is a weed which
has decorative inflated
seed pods with
prickles when setting
seed. Hang up to dry
in a large polythene
bag to hold the seeds
if the pods burst to
stop them spreading.
It is poisonous.

Delphinium
P. * Late Spring/
Summer.
Flowers: wide range of
colours—blue, mauve,
purple, cream, white
and pink. By cutting
back after flowering
to the first leaves on
its stem, secondary
flower stems will be
produced in late
Summer which will be
smaller but easier to
use. *D. ajacis*
(Larkspur): A.
* Summer. Very useful
since a spike-shaped
flower arranges well
with round ones.

Deutzia
D.S. * Summer.
Flowers: white and
pink in June or July
in the garden. Stems
are woody.

Dianthus barbatus
Sweet William. B.
* Late Spring, Summer.
Flowers: old fashioned
and good for cottage-
type arrangements;
long lasting.
● Hammer stems and
remove many of the
basal leaves.

**Dianthus
caryophyllus**
Carnation. P. * All
year round. Garden
flowers in Summer.
Flowers: important
commercial flowers
and there is a tendency
to have dyed ones at
the expense of the old
fashioned varieties;
spray carnations have
three or four flowers
and buds per stem;
border carnations
(pinks) are also very

useful for
arrangements.

Dicentra spectabilis
Bleeding Heart. P.
Late Spring–early
Summer.
Flowers: arching
sprays of bell-like
flowers in a rosy
crimson colour.
Foliage: very
attractive, lacy in
texture, not unlike
aquilegia.

Digitalis
Foxglove. B.
* occasionally.
Summer.
Flowers: useful range
of colours and good-
shaped flower stem for
large groups.
● If stem is hollow, fill
with water: remove
basal leaves and put
into water quickly.

Dimorphotheca
A. * May–October.
Flowers: daisy-type;
two forms available—
D. barberiae purple-
flowered, *D. ecklonis*
white-flowered.
Sometimes they close
up at night.

Dipsacus sylvestris
Teazle. B. * Late
Summer.
Ideal for drying for
Autumn and Winter
arrangements; darker
in colour if left on the
plant to dry naturally.
Found growing wild
in some areas.

Dodecatheon
Relative of the
primula. P. Early
Summer.
Flowers: on a straight
stem of 20–30 cm
(9–12 inches) rising
from a collar of
leaves; ideal for a
small interesting
botanical arrangement
rather than a pretty
one.

Doronicum
Leopard's Bane. P.
* occasionally.
April–May.
Flowers: simple yellow
daisies. The first of a

new range of flowers
after the daffodils,
narcissi and hyacinths
and its different shape
is appreciated at this
time of the year.

Echeveria fulgens
P. Late Spring and
Summer.
Flowers: unusual on
long fleshy stem; long
lasting. Foliage: thick
and fleshy in a thick
rosette; useful as a
focal point for a mixed
green collection. A
very good blue-grey
colour and it goes well
with apricot shades.
● Hammer base of
stem if thick.

Echinops ritro
Globe Thistle. P. July–
August.
Flowers: round blue
flowers on stems of up
to 1 metre (3 feet). A
white form is also
available. Long
lasting, can be dried
for winter use.
Foliage: silver grey-
green and thistle-like.
Very easy to grow.
● Woody stems.

Elaeagnus
E. and D.S. All year
round.
Foliage: often silvery
on underside of leaf;
lasts well in water;
E. pungens aurea and
E. variegata have
yellow margins to
leaves and are
excellent in mixed
foliage groups.
A very worthwhile
foliage to grow.

Embothrium
E.T. May–June and
Autumn.
Flowers: good red
colouring in early
Summer and Autumn.

**Enkianthus
campanulatus**
D.S. May.
Flowers: bell-shaped
at the end of growing
shoots; pale yellow
with some red
markings. Wonderful
Autumn colour.
● Hard woody stem.

**Epimedium
grandiflorum**
P. April–May.
Flowers: stems come
up above the low
ground-covering
foliage with six to
fifteen flowers per
stem; star-like shape
with little spur
projection at back of
flower; pale yellow,
white and violet, and
crimson tipped with
white.

Eranthis
Winter Aconite. Tuber.
Early Spring.
Flowers: yellow in a
rosette of leaves on
very short stem
7–10 cm (3–4 inches);
useful for small moss
gardens.

Eremurus
Foxtail Lily. P.
* Early Summer.
Flowers: white and
pale pink, pale yellow,
and orange; thick
fleshy stems vary in
length from 60 cm to
2 m (2–6 feet); long
lasting and they take
up interesting shapes
after a day or two.
● Need a long drink in
deep buckets.

Erica
Heaths and Heather.
Low-growing E.S.
* Most of the year.
Very many different
varieties. Useful in
small arrangements.
Can be used in small
pots for gardens on a
plate. Can be dried but
does not last long as
bells tend to drop off.
*E. carnea, E. cinerea,
E. × darleyensis,
E. gracilis,
E. mediterranea.
E. vulgaris* syn.
Calluna vulgaris is the
Common Heather.
● Hammer woody
stems.

Erigeron speciosus
Fleabane. P. Summer.
Flowers: daisy-type
with a yellow centre
disc and mauve or rosy
pink outer petals.
● Remove all

unwanted leaves
immediately.

**Eryngium
amethystinum**
P. * July–August.
Flowers: thistle-like;
pretty amethyst
colouring extends to
stem and bracts;
smaller flowers are
pale blue; good for
mixed summer
arrangements and
dried for winter use.
Foliage is striking.

Escallonia
E.S. June–September.
Flowers: tiny trumpet-
shaped in pinks and
white; after the
flowers have finished
the small remaining
seed heads can be used
in a mixed green
arrangement; long
lasting. Foliage: small
glossy leaves.
● Woody stems.

Eschscholzia
Californian Poppy. A.
Summer.
Flowers: bright-
coloured single cone-
shaped poppy—
yellows, orange,
scarlets, apricot,
creams, white.
Foliage is feathery.
● Put in water straight
after cutting.

Eucalyptus
Gum Tree. E.T. * Most
of the year.
Foliage: very useful
and long lasting;
pretty when treated
with glycerine. Fruits
are also good in dried
arrangements.
● Hard woody stems.

Eucomis
Pineapple Flower.
Bulb. * Autumn and
Spring.
Flowers: green flower
spike with purple
markings. A novelty
which looks good for
unusual groups.
● Soft fleshy stem.

Eucryphia glutinosa
Semi-E.S. July–
August.
Flowers: often in

pairs at the end of shoots; white with yellow anthers, about 5 cm (2 inches) diameter; like single roses.

Euonymus japonicus
E. and D.T. and S. * sometimes. All year except when new growth is soft in late Spring.
Foliage: range of variegation, excellent foliage for mixed greens and large arrangements. *E. europaeus* (Spindle Tree): deciduous, magnificent Autumn fruit. *E. radicans*: small-leafed.

Euphorbia
A. and P. * particularly *E. pulcherrima* (Poinsettia) at Christmas. Greenhouse and garden varieties late Spring–Winter. *E. fulgens* is a good cut flower with long arching stems of small orange or white flowers, grown mostly in Holland and Kenya.
● All the family have stems which bleed and need sealing with a flame or boiling water.

Fagus
Beech. D.T. * fresh and glycerined. Spring to Autumn.
Foliage: both green and copper forms are very valuable for backing foliage. The bare branches are good for the framework of shadow leaves (skeletonised magnolia).

Foeniculum vulgare
Fennel. P. Late Summer–mid Autumn.
Foliage: useful for large groups; seed heads good in large mixed green arrangements.
● Hollow stem.

Forsythia
D.S. * February–April.

Flowers: one of the first shrubs to flower; forces well if brought into the house when just in bud; long lasting. Good forms are: *F. intermedia*, *F. ovata*, *F. suspensa*, *F. viridissima*.

Fothergilla major
D.S. April–May, Autumn.
Flowers: rather like off-white bottle brush flowers. Foliage: wonderful Autumn colour.

Freesia
Corm. * Nearly all year round.
Flowers: many beautiful colours, excellent flowers for small arrangements; some double forms are now available, such as 'Diane' white, 'Fantasy' cream.
● Cut stems and place in deep warm water if at all limp.

Fritillaria
Bulb. * *F. imperialis* only. Spring.
A fairly large genus but only two species are commonly grown: *F. imperialis* (Crown Imperial) has a strong smell; useful for large arrangements and Dutch groups but only available for a short time; long lasting. *F. meleagris* (Snake's Head Lily): good on its own or with other small flowers.

Fuchsia
D.S. * as a pot plant. Summer.
Flowers: very elegant when cut and used in vases with a foot— they must hang down to show well; quite long lasting.
● Split stem if woody.

Funkia
syn. *Hosta* (q.v.)

Gaillardia
Blanket Flower.
A. and P. * sometimes. July–September.

Flowers: yellow brown, rather like a helenium; long lasting; they lend themselves to simple mixed arrangements in baskets and heavy stoneware containers.

Galanthus
Snowdrop. Bulb. * January–February.
Flowers: white and some green; double and single varieties, also a giant form; last well in water; pretty on their own in moss with ivy trails for foliage, or in little mixed posies.

Galega
Goat's Rue. P. Summer.
Flowers: white or blue, member of the pea family; good for mixed arrangements.

Galtonia candicans
syn. *Hyacinthus candicans*. Summer Hyacinth. Bulb. July.
Flowers: white, long lasting, good for big groups; individual flowers can be used in a bouquet.
● Treat as soft succulent stems.

Gardenia
E.S. * sometimes. Late Summer.
Flowers: waxy white, highly scented; bruise very easily and go yellow-brown; excellent floating in a shallow crystal dish for a table decoration. Foliage: glossy dark green.

Garrya elliptica
E.S. November–February.
Catkins: silver-grey, male form has the longer catkins; long lasting in water.
● Hard woody stems.

Gaultheria
E.S. * Winter.
Foliage: dark green, long lasting. A number of species available— the most useful have

small-leafed arching sprays.

Gazania splendens
P. Summer–Autumn.
Flowers: colourful daisy-type in yellow, orange and browns; last well. Needs sun to flower well.
Foliage: silvery green with white underside.

Genista
D.S. * as a pot plant. Summer.
Flowers: yellow, long lasting, *G. hispanica* (Spanish Gorse) is good in the garden but not much use cut and is difficult to handle because of spines.
● Hard woody stems.

Gentiana
P. * Spring, September–October.
Many listed in catalogues but the main ones are *G. acaulis* (Spring), intense blue, short stiff stem; *G. sino-ornata* (September–October) deep blue, thin wiry stem, fine leaves; not long lasting but lovely for small arrangements; do not use for decoration under artificial light as the blue colouring will be lost.

Geranium
see *Pelargonium*.

Gerbera jamesonii
Barberton Daisy. P. * All year.
Flowers: daisy-type on long stems in wide range of colours; long lasting; good for modern arrangements. Foliage: not often available.
● Seal cut stems straight away with a flame or boiling water.

Geum
P. Early Summer.
Flowers: simple and good for cottage-type arrangements; double and single forms;

yellow and coppery red.
● Seal tips in a flame.

Gladiolus
Corm. * Summer.
Flowers: very wide range of colours; the small varieties are usually the best for arrangements; last well.
● Cut stems at an angle and remove basal leaves. Some people recommend taking the tip out of the flower stem to encourage the buds to open.

Gloriosa
Torch Lily. Tuber. * as a pot plant or a cut flower imported from Kenya. Summer.
Flowers: very decorative crimson red and yellow flowers on short stems from this climbing greenhouse plant; long lasting; good for exotic arrangements and combines well with fruit.
Foliage: each leaf ends in a tendril.
● Only cut single flower stems.

Godetia
A. * Summer.
Flowers: pretty cottage garden type, rather mallow-like in shape; colours from soft pinks and mauves to crimson.
● Clean off all unwanted foliage, stems may need crushing.

Grevillea
E.T. * Early Spring and Winter. *G. longifolia*: imported from France.
Foliage: often dyed but naturally it has silver and green rather long serrated leaves; fern-like appearance; can be pressed in Autumn. *G. robusta*: used as a pot plant.

Gypsophila elegans
Baby's Breath. A. and

P. * Late Spring–early Autumn.
Flowers: attractive when arranged on their own and good for a hanging basket. *G. elegans*: single white flax-like flower. *G. paniculata* 'Bristol Fairy' is an excellent double form.
● Stems need hammering. Remove all foliage as it soon looks untidy.

Halesia carolina
Snowdrop Tree. D.S. May–June.
Flowers: very pretty white flowers; last well.
● Thin out leaves for a more dramatic effect. Hammer stems.

Hamamelis mollis
Witch Hazel. D.S. * Autumn, Winter.
Flowers: fragrant flowers on bare stems in January and February are very useful for Winter arrangements.
● Woody stems.

Hebe
syn. *Veronica* (q.v.)

Hedera
Ivy. P. All year round.
Foliage: climbing and trailing, used extensively in flower arranging and floristry; very long lasting; some attractive variegated forms.

Helenium
P. * Late Summer–Autumn.
Flowers: daisy-shaped, yellows to reddish browns; seed heads can be dried after flowering. Long lasting in water.

Helianthus
Sunflower. A. and P. * sometimes. Late Summer.
Flowers: clean cut and striking; the annual one is less useful because of its size; long lasting.

Helichrysum
Everlasting. A. * Summer.
Flowers: very important for drying; harvest when young for best results; dry by hanging upside down so stems become straight. Also sold as just flower heads to be glued on to false stems for arranging.

Helipterum roseum
A. * sometimes. Summer.
Grown for drying which is carried out in the same way as for Helichrysum.

Helleborus
P. * November–June.
Range of colour from green, white, pinks to deep purple. Valuable group for the flower arranger. Flowers on single and compound stems.
● Treat tips with boiling water or burn and put straight into water. Some people recommend putting pin pricks all the way up the stem.

Hemerocallis
Day Lily. P. June–September.
Flowers: cream and yellow to brown; flowers tend to open in the late afternoon and stay open until the next day; there are many flowers on each stem so there is a continuity of blooms. Foliage: useful for mixed greens.

Heuchera
Coral Bells. P. May, late Autumn.
Flowers: useful dainty red flower spike. Foliage: short-stemmed leaves go well with other flowers; pretty colouring in late Autumn.

Hippophae
Sea Buckthorn. D.S. Most of the year.
Foliage: silver-grey;

good orange and yellow berries in Autumn and Winter.

Hosta
syn. *Funkia*. P. * April as pot plants, May–August.
Foliage: excellent for the flower arranger with good variegated forms. Flowers: pale lilac, and of secondary importance. Interesting seed spikes for drying if flowers are not picked. The most useful forms are *H. fortunei* 'Marginato Alba', *H. glauca*, *H. sieboldiana*.
● Submerge if soft.

Humulus
Hop. P. Summer.
Often found wild in hedgerows; very decorative and is ideal for Harvest Festival arrangements; dries well for Winter use.

Hyacinthus
Hyacinth. Bulb. * Early December–April/May.
Flowers: many different shades and colours and some double varieties, strongly scented and long lasting when cut; *H. orientalis albulus* (Roman Hyacinths) are the first to flower.
● Place cut hyacinths in a container on their own to allow the thick sap to exude from the stems before arranging with other flowers.

Hyacinthus candicans
syn. *Galtonia candicans* (q.v.)

Hydrangea
D.S. * mostly as pot plants. Summer.
Flowers: white, cream and green, blues, pinks; useful when fresh or dried. *H. macrophylla* is the most common, *H. paniculata* has pointed cream flower heads in September, *H.*

petiolaris is a climber with white flowers.
● If flowers go limp, plunge under water for a few hours to revive. Dry only perfectly formed flowers.

Hypericum
St. John's Wort. E. and D.S. Summer, Autumn.
Flowers: range from pale yellow to deep buttercup colour; many named varieties; long flowering period. Foliage and seed capsule are good in Autumn.
● Remove lower leaves and hammer the stems of the taller shrubs.

Iberis
Candytuft. A. and P. * very occasionally. Late Spring and Summer.
Flowers: white, pinks, mauves; good in simple mixed summer arrangements; annual type have interesting seed heads which dry well; perennial types have woody stems.

Ilex
Holly. E.T. * Cut foliage in December.
Berries: red, orange and yellow berried forms are the most interesting, berries are carried only by females. Foliage: some good variegated forms, many different shaped leaves.
● Keep cut holly in a damp place but do not put stems in water for too long as it tends to drop its leaves when cut and standing in water; if picked in advance, store where birds and mice cannot reach the berries.

Ipomoea
syn. *Pharbitis*. Morning Glory. A. * as a pot plant. Summer.
Flowers: blue, last only a very short time.
● Place tips in boiling

water for a few seconds before arranging.

Iris
Bulbs and tubers. * Winter, Spring, early Summer.
Flowers: divided botanically into eleven groups, covering a wide range of different shapes and sizes. The main ones are listed below:
I. pseudocorus (Flag Iris): short flowering season (May–June) but good seed pods and useful foliage. *I. xiphium* (Dutch, English and Spanish Iris): commercial iris in pale and dark blue, yellow, white and now a few in bronze are available. *I. tuberosa* (Widow Iris), sometimes listed as *Hermodactylus tuberosus*: a good small iris for arranging. *I. unguicularis* syn. *I. stylosa*: first iris of the season, cut when in bud; foliage untidy but flowers go well with jasmine and Christmas roses. *I. reticulata* (Dwarf Iris) and *I. germanica* (Common or Bearded Iris) are the garden iris.

Ixia
Corm. * May–September.
Flowers: attractive spike—habit and foliage like a baby gladiolus; white and blue and violet; very long lasting.
● Cut stems may need hammering.

Jasminum
Semi-E. and D.S. * *J. polyanthum* as a pot plant. Most of the year.
Not long lasting when cut, but flower buds keep opening. *J. nudiflorum* (Winter Jasmine) D. has yellow flowers on long bare stems from November–February. *N. officinale*

(Common jasmine) semi-E. has very fragrant white flowers from June–September. *J. primulinum* E. has yellow flowers March–April.
● Dip stem tips in boiling water.

Juniperus
E.T. Nearly all year. Foliage: used by florists for wreath work but can be good in mixed green arrangements, especially when bearing cones.

Kalenchoe
Pot plant. * December–March, June–July. Flowers: coral or cream in large form (June–July), small flat-headed plants have bright red and cream flowers in Winter which last well when cut. Used a lot in planted arrangements.
● Split stems.

Kalmia
Calico Bush. E.S. or T. * May–June. Flowers: very pretty pink flowers, look like icing sugar flowers.

Kentranthus
Sometimes spelt Centranthus. Valerian. P. Summer. Flowers: usually pink but also available in white and a deep rose; last well.

Kerria japonica
D.S. Spring. Flowers: single or double flowers on long stems with fine foliage. Long lasting when cut. Bare branches useful in Winter months— not unlike Dogwood.

Kniphofia uvaria
Red Hot Poker. P. * July–October. Flowers: take up elegant curves when in water and last well. Foliage: untidy.
● Soft fleshy stems.

Lachenalia aloides
Cape Cowslip. Bulb. * March–April. Flowers: green, red and yellow small flower spikes; long lasting.

Lamium
Dead Nettle. P. Late Spring, Summer. Foliage: more important than flowers; like a short mauve/pink coloured nettle; pretty in small arrangements.

Larix decidua
Larch. D.T. * Spring, Winter. This is the only deciduous cone-bearing tree. Foliage: attractive in young form in Spring. Lasts well in water. Cones: on bare branches in Winter. Also excellent when dead and covered with lichen.
● Put tips of young growth in boiling water.

Lathyrus
Sweet Pea. A. * April (greenhouse)–August. Flowers: pastel shades, not long lasting; best arranged on their own or with a clean cut foliage.
● Never spray the petals unless it is very hot so they will dry quickly—the petals spot and go papery if left wet for a long period. Stems may need splitting if very woody.

Laurus nobilis
Bay. E.S. April–May Foliage: a useful aromatic foliage with interesting green flowers in late Spring.

Lavandula
Lavender. P. * Summer. Flowers: purple spikes with fine scent. Foliage: silver-grey. Not cut a great deal for arrangements but it is a useful shape of

leaf and flower stem for a small vase.

Lavatera
Mallow. A. Summer. Flowers: pink and white, not long lasting but buds open well in water; good for large mixed Summer arrangements.

Leontopodium
Edelweiss. P. June–July. Flowers: silver and grey, ideal to arrange with gentians in a very small vase or on a pewter plate with crystal.

Leucocoryne
Glory of the Sun. B. * Late Spring. Flowers: a form of small lily; pale blue/purple flower spike on stems of 30 cm (1 foot); very fragrant.

Leucojum
Summer Snowflake. Bulb. May–June. Flowers: green and white, ideal for medium-sized arrangements.

Leycesteria formosa
D.S. June–September. Flowers: purple, last quite well. Remove some leaves to show flowers and bracts more clearly.

Liatris
P. * Spring and Summer. Flowers: rose and purple stiff spikes, imported from Holland.
● Stems are very firm and need hammering. Rub off the basal foliage.

Ligustrum
Privet. Mostly E.S. * foliage. Summer and Winter. Foliage: golden form is good in mixed green and Summer arrangements. Berries: black, useful for Winter

arrangements.
● Hammer stems.

Lilium
True Lily. Bulb. * Most of the year. A vast group of flowering plants which last well and make a bold centre to a large group. The main colours are white, yellow, orange and pink. Large numbers are forced in Holland to supply the flower markets. *L. auratum*: July–October; cream and white flowers with yellow and brown spotted petals and a yellow throat—the pollen stains badly so anthers should be removed. *L. candidum* (Madonna Lily): June–July; probably the best known of all lilies; old fashioned upright stems of sweet smelling white waxy petalled flowers, excellent in mixed Summer arrangements; long lasting.
● Remove small leaves which would be below the water line when arranged. Split stems and place in deep buckets for support.

Limonium
Sea Lavender, Statice. P. * Summer, dried in Winter. Flowers: everlasting and more useful dried in Winter than as a cut flower in Summer; tiny deep purple and blue flowers rather like a perennial gypsophila. *L. suworowii* A. * May–June. Flowers: long lilac spike with side branches at base. Foliage: no foliage on stems but flower spikes come from a rosette of leaves.

Linaria
Toadflax. A. and P. July onwards. Flowers: similar to small antirrhinums, on stems 30–45 cm (12–18 ins).

Linum
Flax. A. * sometimes. June–July. Flowers: blue on delicate stem; useful for mixed Summer arrangements.

Lobelia cardinalis
Cardinal Flower. P. Summer. Flowers and foliage: superb red up to 90 cm (3 ft) tall; excellent for mixed red arrangements; last well.
● May require hot water treatment.

Lonicera
Honeysuckle. E. and D.S. Summer and late Winter. *L. fragrantissima*: late Winter. *L. periclymenum*: May–August; sweet smelling and long lasting if cut in bud. *L. nitida* is a useful evergreen foliage with small round deep green leaves. Does not often flower.

Lunaria
Honesty. B. * Seed head form in Autumn and Winter. Flowers: violet and lilac colour. Seed heads: very important but must be harvested before seed pod central membrane becomes stained from the seeds; seed pods are often dyed.
● Hang upside down to dry.

Lupinus polyphyllus
Lupin. P. * occasionally. May–June. Flowers: variety of colours, good on their own or for mixed Summer arrangements.
● Fill hollow stems with water and plug. This will increase their life by one or two days and encourage the stems to take up elegant curves.

Lychnis
syn. *Agrostemma*

Campion. P. Summer.
L. chalcedonica:
scarlet flowers.
L. coronaria: white
woolly shoots at base
and on the purple-
coloured flower spike.
● Soft stem treatment
unless stems are old
and woody; both
varieties are long
lasting.

Macleaya
syn. *Bocconia*. Plume
Poppy. P. Summer.
Foliage: silver and
grey with insignificant
fluffy pink/cream
flowers in July.
● Seal stem tips in
boiling water before
use.

Magnolia
D.T. Late Spring and
Summer.
Flowers: cream and
white, and purple;
blossom is usually out
before foliage and is
subject to frost
damage in late
Spring; best arranged
on their own. *M.
soulangeana* (April):
white with purple
flowers. *M. stellata*:
first to flower, March–
April: star-shaped
flowers. *M. grandiflora*
(August–October):
large water-lily type
flowers.
● Woody stems. The
leaves of *M.
grandiflora* are
excellent dried for
Winter use. Harvest in
the Autumn and press
under the carpet.

Mahonia
E.S. Autumn and
Winter.
Foliage: good colour
in Autumn.
Flowers: Winter and
early Spring, very
fragrant and used in
small arrangements.
M. beali and *M.
'Charity'* are excellent
forms.

Malcolmia maritima
Virginia Stock. A.
Early Summer to
Autumn.
Flowers: very dainty

and sweetly scented;
suitable for small
arrangements.
● Hammer stems if
hard.

Malus
Flowering Crab. D.S.
Spring and Autumn.
Wide range of
flowering trees,
notable species are
M. floribunda and *M.
atrosanguinea*.

Matthiola
Brompton Stock. B.
∗ Spring and Autumn.
Flowers: many shades
from white, cream,
soft pinks, mauves,
purples and apricot on
stiff stems with green
and grey foliage; last
well.
● Stems very woody
and need hot water
treatment. No foliage
must go in water; the
stems are smelly so it
is a good idea to
change the water
frequently.

Megasea
syn. *Bergenia* (q.v.)

Molucella laevis
Bells of Ireland. A.
∗ Summer and in dried
form.
Flowers: the flowers
themselves are
insignificant and it is
the calyx that is the
decorative part:
useful in green
arrangements and
long lasting.
● Warm water
treatment if soft.
Remove all the
leaves.

Monarda didyma
Balm. P. June–
September.
Flowers: decorative
scarlet flowers, good
in mixed garden
arrangements.

Muscari
Grape Hyacinth. Bulb.
∗ March–April.
Flowers: useful small
blue flower which is
long lasting and good
in small arrangements.
Foliage: very untidy

and only the foliage of
M. latifolium is used.
● Soft stems; always
remove any white part
when cutting stems.

Myosotis
Forget-me-not. P.
∗ Spring and Summer.
Flowers: pretty old-
fashioned flowers
which are ideal for
small baskets and
vases of mixed Spring
and Summer flowers.
● Once they have
taken up water they
last well, but the
leaves must be soaked
first; remove many of
the leaves.

Narcissus
Daffodil. Bulb. ∗ Early
November–May.
Flowers: many
varieties available;
best arranged as a
mixture of different
types with their own
foliage and a little
background foliage of
such things as hazel
and berberis; scented
named varieties
include 'Pheasant
Eye' and 'Cheerful-
ness'; miniature
narcissi are good for
small arrangements—
*N. bulbicodium, N.
cyclamineus, N.
jonquilla, N.
juncifolius.*

Nemesia strumosa
A. ∗ as pot plants.
Summer.
Flowers: bright
colours, ideal for small
arrangements and last
quite well.

Nepeta
Catmint. (Nettle
family) P. May–
September.
Flowers: pale
lavender flower spikes.
Foliage: silver and
grey. Very useful in
mixed garden baskets.
● Stems may need
crushing to take up
water.

Nerine
Guernsey Lily. Bulb.
∗ Autumn.
Flowers: hybrids are

now produced in
wonderful colours
from white, pale pink,
through to coral and
scarlet; the old *N.
bowdenii* in hard pink
is the main
commercial variety;
all wonderful in
arrangements and
long lasting.
● Soft fleshy stems.

Nicotiana affinis
Tobacco Plant. A.
Summer.
Flowers: lime green
and white forms are
the most useful;
flowers do not last
long but buds open
well in water and will
replace flowers as they
go over; ideal for
mixed Summer
groups and mixed
green arrangements.
● Stems may need
crushing. Remove all
foliage at and below
the water line.

Nigella
Love-in-the-Mist. A.
∗ Summer.
Flowers: shades of
blue and white in a
collar of feathery
greenery; excellent
seed heads at the end
of the season which
dry well; not long
lasting but buds open
in water.
Remove foliage from
near water line.
N. damascena is a
good form.

Nymphaea
Water Lily. P.
Summer.
Flowers: make an
attractive table
arrangement in a
shallow dish but are
not easy to obtain.
● Keep stems and
leaves right down in
water. To keep the
flowers open, paraffin
wax must be dropped
into the base of the
petals—it should be at
just the right
temperature to run
into the base of the
stem and then set
firmly. If too hot it will
damage the petals.

Oenothera biennis
Evening Primrose. B.
July–September.
Flowers: buds will
open well in water but
flowers are not long
lasting and are best
used in the latter part
of the day. The buds
open freely as the
open flowers fade.
● Hammer any stems
that are woody.

Olearia haastii
New Zealand Daisy
Bush. E.S. July–
August (flowers), all
year (foliage).
Foliage: dark green
with silver back to
leaf.
Flowers: white daisy-
like flowers with
yellow disc; sweet
smelling.
● Woody stems.

**Onopordon
acanthium**
Cotton Thistle. P.
Summer.
Flowers: purple-
flowered heads but
they are prickly so
cruel to handle.
● Put stem tip in very
hot water and give a
good drink before
arranging.

Ornithogalum
Bulb. ∗ sometimes.
Spring and early
Summer.
O. thyrsoides
(Chincherinchee):
white, sometimes
imported at Christmas;
long lasting. *O.
nutans*: green and
white bell-shaped
flower in April and
May. *O. umbellatum*
(Star of Bethlehem):
white star-like flowers
with green and white
backs.
● As tips of stems
become soft, recut—
should last a long time
in water. Flowers from
South Africa may have
tips of stem waxed so
cut off and place in
warm water.

Osmanthus delavayi
E.S. April.
Flowers: small

fragrant white flowers on stiff small-leaved branches, long lasting. *O. ilicifolius* is a dark foliage with small holly-like leaves.

Osmunda regalis
Royal Fern. P. Autumn.
Foliage: excellent Autumn colouring but it is best dried for Winter use, pressed under a carpet.

Paeonia
Peony. P. and D.S. * May–June.
Flowers: white, pink, reds in single or double form, must be picked in bud if they are to last in water; often cold-stored to extend their flowering period; tree paeonies are slow growing and should only be used for special decorations or Japanese style arrangements.
Foliage: good Autumn colour on old leaves.
● Split woody stems. Young foliage can be floated in a bath.

Papaver
Poppy. A. and P.
* *P. nudicaule* Late Spring–early Autumn. *P. orientale*: unusual shades and good for large groups. *P. nudicaule* (Iceland Poppy): colourful reds, orange, yellow, cream and white. *P. rhoeas* (Shirley) and *P. somniferum* (Opium) are in softer shades and usually carry more petals.
● Pick when just showing a trace of colour and burn tips of stems immediately.

Passiflora caerulea
Passion Flower. Climber. * sold as pot plants in shops. Summer.
Flowers: striking but do not last long, especially if stems are short; best floating in a shallow dish.
Foliage: young shoots

are attractive and have tendrils attached.
● Split flower stems.

Pelargonium
Geranium. P. * pot plants. Summer.
Flowers: pinks, reds, mauves and white.
Foliage: small shoots are good for mixed green arrangements or in a goblet of mixed flowers.
● Split stems.

Penstemon
P. Summer.
Flowers: reds, pink and white similar to a small foxglove.
● Stems may need splitting.

Pernettya mucronata
E.S. Early Summer (flowers), Autumn (berries).
Berries: white or pink.
Flowers: only on some varieties, and are like small sprays of lily-of-the-valley.

Petasites fragrans
Winter Heliotrope. P. Early Spring.
Flowers: Vanilla scented; spikes are useful, particularly the green-flowered form *P. japonicus giganteus*.
● Soak foliage before use if it is soft.

Petunia
A. * as a pot plant. Summer.
Flowers: good colour range and useful for a mixed Summer basket but lasting qualities are poor.
● Arrange in warm water.

Phalaris
Ribbon Grass or Gardener's Garters. P. Summer.
Decorative grass, quite pretty when young and growing spikes are used in conjunction with early Spring flowers, not long lasting in water.

● Try putting tips in warm water.

Pharbitis
syn. *Ipomoea* (q.v.)

Philadelphus coronarius
Mock Orange. D.S. June–July.
Flowers: some varieties have masses of white flowers which are highly scented. Range of flower size and shape. Two good varieties are *P. 'Belle Etoile'* and *P. 'Virginal'*. *P. coronarius aureus* has excellent bright yellow foliage in Spring.

Phlomis fruticosa
Jerusalem Sage. E.S. June.
Flowers: pale yellow colouring and rather like a stinging nettle flower.

Phlox
A. and P. Summer.
P. drummondii (A.): long lasting in water and very colourful, self-coloured, bi-coloured and tri-coloured, usually available July–September. *P. paniculata* and *P. × hortorum* (P.) have a sweet scent in early Autumn; many pink and mauve shades and white; last well; stems woody.

Phormium tenax
New Zealand Flax. P. Summer.
Foliage: very striking spear-shaped leaf up to 2 metres (7 ft) long; good for large arrangements or mixed greens. *P. tenax variegatum* has a striped yellow and green leaf. *P. tenax veitchii* has creamy white stripes.

Phygelius capensis
Cape Figwort. E.S. Late Summer.
Flowers: scarlet flowers make interesting material

for a red group.
● Split stems and stand in warm water.

Physalis franchetii
Chinese Lantern. P. * fresh or dried. Early Summer (fresh).
Ideal for drying for Winter decoration but can be used in its fresh state.
● Remove most of the leaves.

Physostegia virginiana
Obedient Plant. P. * August–September.
Flowers: purple or white, long lasting; can be placed in certain positions on the stem and will remain there, hence the plant's common name.
● Woody stems, remove many of the leaves up the square stem.

Phytolacca americana
Red Ink Plant. P. Late Summer.
Berries: dark purple and stain badly; berries and roots are poisonous. May be used in its early stage when green or later when coloured.
● Remove most of the leaves.

Pieris floribunda
syn. *Andromeda floribunda*. Lily-of-the-Valley Tree. E.S. * March–May.
Flowers: Like lily-of-the-valley sprays. *P. japonica* has larger sprays. *P. formosa* has young scarlet growth at the tips of foliage. Foliage lasts well.

Pinus
Pine. E.T. * sometimes. Autumn and Winter.
Cones: branches carrying cones are very useful for Winter decorations. Many different forms and a wide colour range. The blue is the most popular.

Pittosporum tenuifolium
E.T. * October–April.
Foliage: long lasting glossy small round leaves with wavy edges; important commercial crop.

Platycodon grandiflorus
Chinese Bell Flower. P. Summer.
Flowers: white and blue; stem lengths up to 60 cm (2 feet).
● Stems tend to bleed —seal in a flame and get them into water straight away.

Polygonatum multiflorum
Solomon's Seal. P. * May to June.
Foliage: arching stems carrying little tubular white and green flowers; long lasting in water. The leaves can be used on their own after the flowers have finished.
● Cut at an angle and allow a deep drink before use.

Polygonum baldschuanicum
Russian Vine. D. Climber. July–October.
Flowers: small sprays of flowers can be cut and used in candle cup arrangements.
● Soak well before use.

Potentilla fruticosa
E.S. June–August.
Flowers: small yellow single rose-like; last well.
● Hammer woody stems.

Primula
P. * March–June and Autumn.
Popular garden plants are *P. auricula*, *P. denticulata*, *P. japonica* and *P. polyanthus*.
● *P. polyanthus* sometimes wilt so get into deep water straight away and prick right down the stem. *P. auricula* and

P. denticulata
normally take up
water well.

Prunus
Plum, Cherry, Peach
and Apricot. D.T.
Spring (flowers),
Autumn (fruit).
P. laurocerasus (E.) is
the Common Laurel.
*P. subhirtilla
autumnalis* flowers in
October–November.

**Pulmonaria
officinalis**
Jerusalem Cowslip,
Soldiers and Sailors.
P. Spring.
Flowers: pink, turning
to a purple-blue; often
used in mixed Spring
arrangements with
primroses, polyanthus,
heathers; quite long
lasting. Foliage:
spotted.

Pulsatilla vulgaris
syn. *Anemone
pulsatilla*. Pasque
Flower. P. Spring,
Early Summer.
Flowers: pale mauve;
P. alpina sulphurea
has pale yellow
flowers in May and
June. Seed heads are
most attractive to use
with mixed greens in
summer.
● Place flowers in deep
water before
arranging.

Pyracantha
Firethorn. E.S. May
(flowers), Autumn
(berries). Flowers:
white. Berries: red,
orange-yellow and will
last all Winter.
● Woody stems and
remove spiteful
thorns.

Pyrethrum
A form of
Chrysanthemum. P.
* Early Summer.
Flowers: single-daisy
type in red and pink
with yellow centre
disc; quite long
lasting.

Ranunculus
Buttercup family. P.
* Spring and Summer.

Flowers: many bright
colours; good for
arrangements and
long lasting; as
flowers open, the
weight makes them
take up attractive
curves. *R. asiaticus* is
the usual commercial
flower.
● Allow plenty of
water as the heads are
heavy and can
fracture stems if they
bend over when limp.

Reseda
Mignonette. P. June–
October.
Flowers: green and
yellow with a little
white, look rather like
millet; they are
sweet-scented and
used to feature in tied
nosegays.

Rheum palmatum
Rhubarb family. P.
Summer.
Foliage: large leaves
used in very big
groups. Flowers: like
the wild dock in deep
red; not often grown.
● Submerge leaves
before use as they
easily become soft.

**Rhododendron and
Azalea**
E. and D.S. November–
August.
Important group of
shrubs and trees, wide
range of colours in
white, cream, pale
yellow, pinks, reds
and purples; last up to
ten days if cut in bud.

Rhus cotinus
Smoke Tree. D.S.
Autumn.
Foliage: useful colour
and has a smoke-grey
effect from the spent
flower stems in
Autumn. *R. typhina*
(Stag's Horn Sumach):
pyramidal flower
panicles, wonderful
Autumn colour.

Ribes
Flowering Currant.
D.S. Spring.
R. sanguineum:
flowers in deep pink,
hang down like

clusters of grapes
before much of the
foliage has opened;
long lasting but it has
a strong unpleasant
smell when cut in the
house. There are
named varieties with
white and yellow
flowers in this species.
● Treat as woody
stems.

Rodgersia pinnata
P. June–July.
Flowers: white or rose
pink with flat heads.
● Hollow stem.

Romneya
P. Summer.
Flowers: like a large
single white poppy
with grey-green
foliage, sometimes
mistaken for a paeony.

Rosa
D.S. May–July and
Autumn (garden), all
year round (commer-
cial crop).
Many different
varieties, forms and
colours. Important as
a garden flower,
commercial crop, and
excellent for the
flower arranger.
● Remove thorns
except for a single rose
in a specimen vase,
cut and hammer stems,
and put stem tips in
boiling water. Recut
and repeat treatment
if they show signs of
wilting.

**Rosmarinus
officinalis**
Rosemary. E.S.
* sometimes. Summer
and Autumn.
Foliage: silver grey
back to dark green
narrow leaves, very
fragrant.

Rudbeckia
P. July–September.
Flowers: yellow and
brown colours, daisy
like, long lasting when
cut. Most common
forms are *R. hirta*
(Black-eyed Susan)
and *R. laciniata* (Cone
Flower).
● Hammer thick stems.

Ruscus aculeatus
Butcher's Broom. E.S.
* dried and dyed.
Rarely used in its
natural form but
female plants can be
quite attractive when
carrying berries.
● Very hard woody
stem.

Ruta graveolens
Rue. E.S. Summer.
Foliage: small and
useful in pretty green
and grey colouring;
smell is sometimes
thought to be
unpleasant. Flowers:
not significant but can
be used. Young
foliage is best in May–
October.

Salix
Willow. D.T. * Late
Winter, early Spring.
S. babylonica (Weeping
Willow): beautiful in
Spring when just
breaking. *S. medemii*:
excellent for early
catkins. Pussy willow
bare branches are very
popular during late
Winter. *S. matsudana*
'Tortuosa' (Contorted
Willow) is often grown
for use in early Spring.

Salpiglossis sinuata
A. Summer.
Flowers: colourful and
resemble the
convolvulus flower in
shape; good for mixed
arrangements.

Salvia
Sage. A. and P. * as a
pot plant. Summer.
Flowers: red, and blue
and purple. Foliage:
strongly scented soft
grey and green. Good
forms are: *S. sclarea*
(Clary), *S. splendens*
(Scarlet Sage).

Sansevieria
Mother-in-law's
Tongue. Pot plant.
* All year.
A leaf will last well in
an arrangement and
can take the place of
an iris or phormium
leaf in a mixed green
group. Leaves have
attractive markings.

Santolina
Lavender Cotton. E.S.
July.
Foliage: silver-grey
with yellow flower
heads in July; rather a
pungent smell.
● Place in water
straight away as it
wilts quickly; plunge
before use for a few
hours if necessary.

Scabiosa
Scabious. A. and P.
* Summer.
S. caucasica (P.) are
blues and sometimes
white form. *S.
atropurpurea* (A.) are a
wide range of blue,
purple and deep red,
and last well in water.
S. elata syn.
Cephalaria tatarica is
the yellow perennial
scabious and is also
useful.

Schizanthus
Poor Man's Orchid. A.
May–August.
Pretty foliage and a
wide range of flower
colours.

Schizostylis
Kaffir Lily. P.
* Autumn.
Member of the iris
family. *S.* 'Viscountess
Byng' (pink) is the
main form.

Scilla
Bluebell and Wild
Hyacinth. Bulb.
* sometimes. Late
Spring.
Flowers: useful for
small arrangements in
late Spring but do not
last long.

Sedum
P. * Summer and
Autumn.
Large group of rock
garden plants, the
most popular varieties
are: *S. sieboldii*
'Medio-variegatum':
round flat fleshy
leaves with a yellow
blotch, useful for
small arrangements.
*S. spectabile
atropurpureum*
'Brilliant' has
excellent large pink

148

flower heads in Autumn.

Sempervivum
Houseleek. P. Summer.
Foliage: rosette of thick fleshy leaves can be used to good effect in the centre of a small mixed green. Flowers: star-like, can be useful for a special arrangement.

Senecio laxifolius
E.S. All year round except January and February.
Foliage: silver-grey with white backs to the leaves. Flowers: yellow daisy-like on silvery spikes. July. *S. cineraria* syn. *Cineraria maritima* (q.v.)

Sidalcea
Mallow family. P. Summer.
Flowers: pink and purple. Foliage: pretty for a mixed Summer arrangement.

Silybum
Milk Thistle. B. Summer.
Foliage: beautifully marked. Flowers: rose and purple in Summer.
● Leaves need boiling water treatment. It is a good idea to float them in a bowl of water before use.

Smilacina racemosa
P. May.
Foliage: similar to Solomon's Seal. Flowers: feathery cluster at the end of the leaf spike; fragrant.

Solanum capsicastrum
Winter Cherry. P. * as a pot plant. Winter.
Berries: red; flowers must be pollinated by August if berries are to form and ripen for Christmas. Remove a few leaves to allow berries to show to advantage.
● Woody stem.

Solidago
Golden Rod. P. August–September.
Flowers: arching sprays of yellow flowers which can vary in colour if a range of varieties is grown; seed heads are also useful.
● Woody stems. Remove many of the lower leaves.

Sorbus
D.T. Spring and Autumn.
S. aria (Whitebeam): beautiful silver foliage in April and May, and good Autumn fruit; the elegant branches last well when cut. *S. aucuparia* (Rowan or Mountain Ash). good Autumn fruit.

Spartium junceum
Spanish Broom. D.S. June–September.
Flowers: yellow pea shaped flowers similar to common broom but larger and less crowded. Lasts well when cut.
● Hammer stems.

Spiraea
D.S. Spring and June–September.
Wide range of foliage and flowers: *S. arguta*: white, April–May. *S. douglasii*: purple and rose, June–July. *S. japonica*: rose and red, June–July. *S. veitchii*: white flowers, long arching branches, June–July.

Stachys lanata
Lamb's Ears, Lamb's Tongue. P. June.
Foliage: low growing with soft grey felty leaves which can be used for most of the year. Flowers: flower spike is useful for extra length on foliage stem just before it opens in July and it can be dried.
● Do not allow foliage to become soaked or it will act as a syphon. Tips may be burnt.

Stephanotis
Madagascar Jasmine. P. * April–November.
Flowers: wax-like tubular and star-shaped white flowers with a very strong smell; long lasting; good for table bowl decorations where short stems are required.

Strelitzia
Bird of Paradise. P. * Imported from Kenya.
Foliage: good but not readily available. Flowers: very exotic and are used for special effects; long lasting.
● Give a long drink before use.

Symphoricarpos
Snowberry. D.S. * Autumn.
Foliage: oval-shaped leaves on arching sprays with opaque berries at the tips in white or pink. The variety 'Constance Spry' is excellent. Lasts extremely well in water.

Syringa
Lilac. D.S. * May–June and forced from Holland, December–March.
Flowers: white, pink and mauve, lilac, deep purple.
● Woody stems, remove all leaves from flower stem but keep some short foliage shoots to arrange in amongst the bare stems.

Tagetes
African and French Marigolds. * African Marigolds on single stems up to 30 cm (12 inches). Summer.
Flowers: orange, yellow, brown and have a strong smell which can be unpleasant in the house.
● Cut stems, remove basal leaves and place in warm water.

Taxus
Yew. E.T. Autumn–Winter.
Foliage: useful backing for large groups in Winter months; long lasting; attractive variegated form. Berries are poisonous.
● Hammer well.

Thalictrum dipterocarpum
Meadow Rue. P. Summer.
Foliage: very attractive for mixed garden flower arrangements, similar to aquilegia; *T. dipterocarpum* 'Hewitt's Double' is attractive but a little untidy and is best used in small pieces rather than the large stem.

Tilia
Lime. D.T. Spring.
Foliage: young lime is very beautiful in Spring as background foliage and stripped lime is excellent— remove all the leaves from the branches so that just the flowers and bracts remain. Popular forms are *T. europaea* (Common Lime) and *T. petiolaris* (Pendant Silver Lime).

Tradescantia
P. * *T. fluminensia* (Wandering Jew). Summer.
Foliage: coloured forms in silver, purple and gold are the most popular. Flowers: rather insignificant and not widely used. The herbaceous plant *T. virginiana* has useful flower stems in July and August but foliage is not good for arranging.

Tritonia
Montbretia. Corm. May–June.
Flowers: mostly orange colours; long lasting. Foliage: iris-like.
● Place cut stems in deep water.

Trollius europaeus
Globe Flower. P. * Early June.
Flowers: yellow like a giant buttercup, not long lasting but a good shape and foliage is interesting.
● Cut when young and get into water straight away.

Tropaeolum majus
Nasturtium. A. Summer.
Flowers: good colours and last quite well when cut; best varieties are those with double flowers.

Tulipa
Tulip. Bulb. * December–May.
Flowers: wide range of colours; flowers take up beautiful curves in water; lily-flowered and double tulips are very useful.
● Wrap flowers in stiff paper and give a long drink to ensure that flower heads do not droop and break the delicate stem. Some people recommend pricking through the stem under the flower head with a pin to enable tulips to take up water better.

Typha
Reed Mace, Bulrush. P. * Autumn for seed heads.
Foliage: useful for backing large Summer groups. Flowers: brown cylindrical head.
● Cut flower before it is really ripe and spray with hair lacquer to stop it splitting.

Vallota speciosa
Scarborough Lily. Bulb. * sometimes. September–October.
Flowers: three or four scarlet flowers at the top of the thick fleshy stem; similar to a small Amaryllis; long lasting.
● Thick fleshy stems.

Verbascum

Mullein. B. June onwards.
Flowers: interesting flower spike with pale yellow flowers on a thick hairy stem; useful in mixed Summer groups. Foliage: large hairy soft leaves.
● Put in warm water if it begins to wilt. The seed heads dry well if hung upside down and being tall they make a useful backing for arrangements.

Verbena

A. and P. Summer.
Flowers: good colour range in the annual form. Flowers: flat heads, long lasting and good for mixed Summer groups; best perennial forms are *V. bonariensis* and *V. canadensis*.
● Split stems if at all woody.

Veronica

syn. *Hebe* in shrubby form. E.S. form and P. border plants. Summer. Very large genus.
Foliage: wide range of leaf shape and colour, useful for mixed greens; the smallest form *V. buchananii* is one of the most useful species. Flowers: loose spikes of blue, pale pinks or white colouring.
● Woody stems.

Viburnum

Snowball Tree, Wayfaring Tree. D.S. and T. All year round from different varieties.
Flowers: fragrant, usually white or pink in flat heads; some early flowers catch the frost. Foliage: takes good colour in Autumn. Best hybrids are *V.* × *bodnantense*, *V.* × *burkwoodii*, and best species are *V. carlesii*, *V. fragrans* and *V. opulus* (Guelder Rose).

Vinca

Periwinkle. P. Late Spring.
Foliage: long trailing stems of oval leaves with yellow margins; variegated form is useful. Flowers: blue; of secondary importance.
● Split stems.

Viola

Violet. P. * 'Princess of Wales' (September–October) and 'Herrick' (March–April) only.
Flowers: garden varieties of viola are useful for table bowls and small vases. *V. tricolor* is the plant that the garden pansy has been derived from. When cut it can only be used for small posies.
● *V. odorata* (True Violet) drink through their heads and should always be kept moist.

Viscum album

Mistletoe. P. (parasitic). * Winter.
Useful at Christmas; it looks attractive just glittered with variegated holly and ivy in a low bowl. It is unwise to encourage mistletoe in the garden as it will kill trees.

Vitis

Vine. P. Autumn.
Foliage: interesting shaped leaves with good colour in Autumn (Autumn colour comes at the end of their life). *V. coignetiae* is recommended.
● Dip tips of leaves in boiling water, but leaves do not last long.

Watsonia

Corm. August–September.
Flowers: very elegant spikes, like a fine flowered gladiolus, white and pale pink with some scarlet and crimson.
● As *Gladiolus*.

Wisteria

Climber. Late Spring–early Summer.
Lasts only a very short time when cut. Needs to be used in a vase on a stem so that the flowers hang down.
● Place tips in boiling water to hold flowers.

Yucca

E.S. Summer.
Flowers: useful for a really striking large group. Foliage: individual leaves can be cut to take the place of large Phormium or Cordyline.

Zantedeschia aethiopica

syn. *Calla aethiopica*. Arum Lily, Lords and Ladies. P. * December–April, outdoor crop July–August.
Flowers: green form is very popular; the yellow *Z. elliotiana* and the little pink and cream Arum *Z. rehmanii* are imported, usually in Spring.
● Soft fleshy stem.

Zinnia elegans

A. Summer–Autumn.
Flowers: good colours; subject to heads bending over at the top of the flower stem. This flower is sometimes wired internally when purchased from the florist to hold the heavy flower head in position.
● Place tips in hot water then give a good drink in warm water before arranging. In large varieties the stem is hollow and should be filled with warm water.

PAGES 136–7 A collection of interesting and exotic plant materials, including *Anthurium, Strelitzia, Chincherinchee, Cyclamen, Plumbago, Abutilon, Cymbidium* (orchid), *Primula malacoides*.
BELOW A late Winter arrangement combining the charm of snowdrops with the wonderfully scented *Chimonanthus fragrans*. Also included are *Hamamelis, Hedera* and some moss and cork bark for interest.

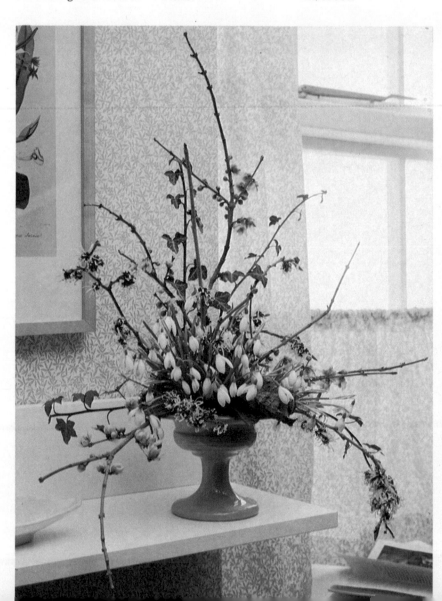

Cross reference chart
Common names to general

Common name	Genus	Common name	Genus	Common name	Genus
African Lily	*Agapanthus*	Coral Bells	*Heuchera*	Houseleek	*Sempervivum*
Alder	*Alnus*	Cornelian Cherry	*Cornus*	Hyacinth, Grape	*Muscari*
Angel's Trumpet	*Datura*	Cornflower	*Centaurea*	Hyacinth, Summer	*Galtonia*
Apricot	*Prunus*	Cotton Thistle	*Onopordon*	Hyacinth, Wild	*Scilla*
Artichoke	*Cynara*	Cowslip, Cape	*Lachenalia*		
Arum Lily	*Zantedeschia*	Cowslip, Jerusalem	*Pulmonaria*	Iceland Poppy	*Papaver*
Ash, Mountain	*Sorbus*	Crab, Flowering	*Malus*	Ivy	*Hedera*
Aster, China	*Callistephus*	Crocus, Autumn	*Colchicum*		
Autumn Crocus	*Colchicum*	Crown Imperial	*Fritillaria*	Japonica	*Chaenomeles*
		Cup and Saucer Plant	*Cobaea*	Jasmine	*Jasminum*
Baby's Breath	*Gypsophila*	Cupid's Dart	*Catananche*	Jasmine, Madagascar	*Stephanotis*
Balm	*Monarda*	Currant, Flowering	*Ribes*	Jerusalem Cowslip	*Pulmonaria*
Bamboo	*Arundinaria*			Jerusalem Sage	*Phlomis*
Barberry	*Berberis*	Daffodil	*Narcissus*	Jonquil	*Narcissus*
Barberton Daisy	*Gerbera*	Daisy, Barberton	*Gerbera*		
Bay	*Laurus*	Daisy, Michaelmas	*Aster*	Kaffir Lily	*Schizostylis*
Bear's Breeches	*Acanthus*	Daisy, Shasta	*Chrysanthemum*		
Beech	*Fagus*	Day Lily	*Hemerocallis*	Lady's Mantle	*Alchemilla*
Bell Flower, Chinese	*Platycodon*	Dead Nettle	*Lamium*	Lamb's Ears	*Stachys*
Belladonna Lily	*Amaryllis*	Dogwood	*Cornus*	Lamb's Tongue	*Stachys*
Bellflower	*Campanula*			Larch	*Larix*
Bells of Ireland	*Molucella*	Edelweiss	*Leontopodium*	Larkspur	*Delphinium*
Birch	*Betula*	Elephant's Ears	*Bergenia*	Laurel, Common	*Prunus*
Bird of Paradise	*Strelitzia*	Evening Primrose	*Oenothera*	Laurel, Spotted	*Aucuba*
Black-eyed Susan	*Rudbeckia*	Everlasting Flowers	*Helichrysum, Limonium*	Lavender	*Lavandula*
Bladder Senna	*Colutea*			Lavender Cotton	*Santolina*
Blanket Flower	*Gaillardia*	Fennel	*Foeniculum*	Lavender, Sea	*Limonium*
Bleeding Heart	*Dicentra*	Fern, Maidenhair	*Adiantum*	Leopard's Bane	*Doronicum*
Bluebell	*Scilla*	Fern, Royal	*Osmunda*	Lilac	*Syringa*
Bottle Brush	*Callistemon*	Figwort, Cape	*Phygelius*	Lily	*Lilium*
Box	*Buxus*	Firethorn	*Pyracantha*	Lily, African	*Agapanthus*
Brompton Stock	*Matthiola*	Flamingo Flower	*Anthurium*	Lily, Arum	*Zantedeschia*
Broom	*Cytisus*	Flax	*Linum*	Lily, Belladonna	*Amaryllis*
Broom, Butcher's	*Ruscus*	Flax, New Zealand	*Phormium*	Lily, Candidum	*Lilium*
Broom, Spanish	*Spartium*	Fleabane	*Erigeron*	Lily, Day	*Hemerocallis*
Buckthorn, Sea	*Hippophae*	Flowering Currant	*Ribes*	Lily, Foxtail	*Eremurus*
Bulrush	*Typha*	Forget-me-not	*Myosotis*	Lily, Guernsey	*Nerine*
Bunny's Ears	*Stachys*	Foxglove	*Digitalis*	Lily, Kaffir	*Schizostylis*
Butcher's Broom	*Ruscus*	Foxtail Lily	*Eremurus*	Lily, Madonna	*Lilium*
Buttercup	*Ranunculus*	French Marigold	*Tagetes*	Lily, Peruvian	*Alstroemeria*
				Lily, Scarborough	*Vallota*
Calico Bush	*Kalmia*	Gardener's Garters	*Phalaris*	Lily, Snake's Head	*Fritillaria*
Californian Poppy	*Eschscholzia*	Geranium	*Pelargonium*	Lily, Tiger	*Lilium*
Camomile	*Anthemis*	Globe Flower	*Trollius*	Lily, Torch	*Gloriosa*
Campion	*Lychnis*	Globe Thistle	*Echinops*	Lily, Water	*Nymphaea*
Candidum Lily	*Lilium*	Glory of the Sun	*Leucocoryne*	Lily-of-the-Valley	*Convallaria*
Candytuft	*Iberis*	Goat's Beard, False	*Astilbe*	Lily-of-the-Valley Tree	*Pieris*
Canterbury Bell	*Campanula*	Goat's Rue	*Galega*	Lime	*Tilia*
Cape Cowslip	*Lachenalia*	Golden Rod	*Solidago*	Lords and Ladies	*Zantedeschia*
Cape Figwort	*Phygelius*	Gorse, Spanish	*Genista*	Love-in-the-Mist	*Nigella*
Cardinal Flower	*Lobelia*	Gourd	*Cucurbita*	Love-lies-bleeding	*Amaranthus*
Cardoon	*Cynara*	Grape Hyacinth	*Muscari*	Lupin	*Lupinus*
Carnation	*Dianthus*	Guelder Rose	*Viburnum*		
Catmint	*Nepeta*	Guernsey Lily	*Nerine*	Madagascar Jasmine	*Stephanotis*
Cherry	*Prunus*	Gum Tree	*Eucalyptus*	Madonna Lily	*Lilium*
Cherry, Cornelian	*Cornus*			Maidenhair Fern	*Adiantum*
Cherry, Winter	*Solanum*	Hawthorn	*Crataegus*	Mallow	*Lavatera*
China Aster	*Callistephus*	Hazel	*Corylus*	Maple	*Acer*
Chincherinchee	*Ornithogalum*	Heaths and Heather	*Erica*	Marigold	*Calendula*
Chinese Bell Flower	*Platycodon*	Heliotrope, Winter	*Petasites*	Marigold, African and French	*Tagetes*
Chinese Lantern	*Physalis*	Holly	*Ilex*		
Christmas Rose	*Helleborus*	Holly, Sea	*Eryngium*	May	*Crataegus*
Clary	*Salvia*	Hollyhock	*Althaea*	Meadow Rue	*Thalictrum*
Columbine	*Aquilegia*	Honesty	*Lunaria*	Mexican Orange Blossom	*Choisya*
Cone Flower	*Rudbeckia*	Honeysuckle	*Lonicera*	Michaelmas Daisy	*Aster*
Convolvus	*Ipomoea*	Hop	*Humulus*	Mignonette	*Reseda*
		Hornbeam	*Carpinus*		

Milk Thistle	*Silybum*	St. John's Wort	*Hypericum*	Thistle, Milk	*Silybum*
Mimosa	*Acacia*	Saxifrage, Giant	*Bergenia*	Thorn Apple	*Datura*
Mistletoe	*Viscum*	Scabious	*Scabiosa*	Thrift	*Armeria*
Mock Orange	*Philadelphus*	Scarborough Lily	*Vallota*	Tiger Lily	*Lilium*
Monkshood	*Aconitum*	Scarlet Sage	*Salvia*	Toadflax	*Linaria*
Montbretia	*Tritonia*	Sea Buckthorn	*Hippophae*	Tobacco Plant	*Nicotiana*
Montbretia, Garden	*Crocosmia*	Sea Holly	*Eryngium*	Torch Lily	*Gloriosa*
Morning Glory	*Ipomoea*	Sea Lavender	*Limonium*	True Lily	*Lilium*
Mother-in-law's Tongue	*Sansevieria*	Shasta Daisy	*Chrysanthemum*	Tuberose	*Polianthes*
		Shirley Poppy	*Papaver*	Tulip	*Tulipa*
Mountain Ash	*Sorbus*	Smilax	*Asparagus*	Turk's Cap	*Lilium*
Mouse Plant	*Arisarum*	Smoke Tree	*Rhus*		
Mullein	*Verbascum*	Snake's Head Lily	*Fritillaria*	Umbrella Plant	*Cyperus*
		Snapdragon	*Antirrhinum*		
Nasturtium	*Tropaeolum*	Snowball Tree	*Viburnum*	Valerian	*Kentranthus*
Nettle, Dead	*Lamium*	Snowberry	*Symphoricarpos*	Vine	*Vitis*
New Zealand Daisy Bush	*Olearia*	Snowdrop	*Galanthus*	Vine, Russian	*Polygonum*
		Snowdrop Tree	*Halesia*	Violet	*Viola*
New Zealand Flax	*Phormium*	Snowflake, Summer	*Leucojum*	Virginia Stock	*Malcolmia*
		Soldiers and Sailors	*Pulmonaria*		
Obedient Plant	*Physostegia*			Wallflower	*Cheiranthus*
Opium Poppy	*Papaver*	Solomon's Seal	*Polygonatum*	Wandering Jew	*Tradescantia*
Orach	*Atriplex*	Southernwood	*Artemisia*	Water Lily	*Nymphaea*
Orchid, Poor Man's	*Schizanthus*	Spanish Broom	*Spartium*	Wayfaring Tree	*Viburnum*
		Spanish Gorse	*Genista*	Whitebeam	*Sorbus*
Pampas Grass	*Cortaderia*	Spindle Tree	*Euonymus*	Willow	*Salix*
Pasque Flower	*Pulsatilla*	Spotted Laurel	*Aucuba*	Winter Aconite	*Eranthis*
Passion Flower	*Passiflora*	Stag's Horn Sumach	*Rhus*	Winter Cherry	*Solanum*
Peach	*Prunus*			Winter Heliotrope	*Petasites*
Pendant Silver Lime	*Tilia*	Star of Bethlehem	*Ornithogalum*	Wintersweet	*Chimonanthus*
Periwinkle	*Vinca*	Statice	*Limonium*	Witch Hazel	*Hamamelis*
Peruvian Lily	*Alstroemeria*	Stock, Brompton	*Matthiola*	Wormwood	*Artemisia*
Pine	*Pinus*	Stock, Virginia	*Malcolmia*		
Pineapple Flower	*Eucomis*	Strawberry Tree	*Arbutus*	Yarrow	*Achillea*
Pinks	*Dianthus*	Summer Hyacinth	*Galtonia*	Yew	*Taxus*
Plum	*Prunus*	Summer Snowflake	*Leucojum*		
Plume Poppy	*Macleaya*	Sunflower	*Helianthus*		
Poinsettia	*Euphorbia*	Sweet Pea	*Lathyrus*		
Poor Man's Orchid	*Schizanthus*	Sweet Sultan	*Centaurea*		
Poppy, Californian	*Eschscholzia*	Sweet William	*Dianthus*		
Poppy, Iceland	*Papaver*				
Poppy, Opium	*Papaver*	Teazle	*Dipsacus*		
Poppy, Plume	*Macleaya*	Thistle	*Onopordon*		
Poppy, Shirley	*Papaver*	Thistle, Globe	*Trollius*		
Pot Marigold	*Calendula*				
Primrose, Evening	*Oenothera*				
Privet	*Ligustrum*				
Pussy Willow	*Salix*				
Quaking Grass	*Briza*				
Quince	*Chaenomeles*				
Red Hot Poker	*Kniphofia*				
Red Ink Plant	*Phytolacca*				
Reed Mace	*Typha*				
Rhubarb	*Rheum*				
Ribbon Grass	*Phalaris*				
Rose	*Rosa*				
Rose, Christmas	*Helleborus*				
Rose, Guelder	*Viburnum*				
Rosemary	*Rosmarinus*				
Rowan	*Sorbus*				
Royal Fern	*Osmunda*				
Rue	*Ruta*				
Rue, Goat's	*Galega*				
Rue, Meadow	*Thalictrum*				
Russian Vine	*Polygonum*				
Sage	*Salvia*				
Sage, Jerusalem	*Phlomis*				

BELOW Mimosa makes an attractive decoration but does not last well.

RIGHT A mixed green arrangement in a round wicker basket.

INDEX

(Figures in italics refer to the captions)

A

Abutilon 138, *150*
Acacia 12, 27, 138, *152*
Acanthus mollis 138; to dry 134
Acer 19, 138
Achillea 50, *79*, 87, 138; to dry 134
Acidanthera 138
Aconite, Winter see Eranthis
Aconitum 138
Acroclinium *132*; to dry 134
Adiantum *114*, 138
Aegillea 97
African Lily see Agapanthus
African Marigold see Tagetes
Agapanthus 87, 138
Ageratum 89
Agrostemma see Lychnis
Ajuga atropurpurea variegata 66
Alabaster vases 31, *72*, 78
Alchemilla mollis 19, *39*, 70, *70*, 72, *72*, *79*, *81*, *121*, 138
Alder see Alnus
Allium *33*, 74, *79*, *83*, 117, *117*, 138; to dry 134
Alnus 19, 100, *100*, *121*, 138
Alstroemeria 45, *97*, *121*, 138
Althaea rosea 25, 138
Alyssum saxatile 55
Amaranthus caudatus *23*, *38*, *39*, *53*, 87, *97*, 138; to dry 134
Amaryllis 25, *25*, *90*, 138
Amelanchier 138
Anchusa 138
Andromeda floribunda see Pieris floribunda
Anemone 12, *89*, 92, *92*, 117, *117*, 138–9; A. pulsatilla see Pulsatilla vulgaris
Angelica 70, 139
Angel's Trumpet see Datura
Anthemis 139
Anthurium 139, *150*
Antirrhinum *53*, 59, 72, *72*, *79*, 88, *88*, *97*, *97*, *124*, *128*, 139
Apricot see Prunus
Aquilegia *51*, 139

Aralia 19, *83*, 139
Arbutus 19, 100, *121*, 139
Arctotis 139
Arisarum 59, 139
Armeria 139
Arrangements, flower: autumn 86–97; for children 116–17; for churches 123–9; large 121–2; for a party 55; room 54–5; special 120–9, spring 58–67, summer 70–83; table 55, 59, 66; winter 100–7; see also Flowers
Artemisia 19, 139
Artichoke see Cynara scolymus
Arum italicum pictum 19, 72, *72*, 139
Arum Lily see Zantedeschia
Aruncus 38
Arundinaria 19, 139
Asclepias physocarpa 90
Asparagus 65, *79*, 139
Aspidistra elatior variegata 60, *61*, 139
Asplenium 139
Aster *35*, 87, *89*, 139
Aster, China see Callistephus
Astilbe 139
Astrantia 9, *92*, *102*, 139
Atriplex *53*, 94, *94*, *97*, 139; to dry 134
Aucuba 9, 19, *100*, 139
Auricula 139
Autumn Crocus see Colchicum
Autumn flowers 86–97
Azalea *16*, 58, *86*, 94, *94*, 100, *103*, *124*, 139, 148

B

Baby's Breath see Gypsophila
Bacteria 22, 23
Ballota pseudodictamnus 79
Balm see Monarda didyma
Bamboo see Arundinaria
Barberry see Berberis
Barberton Daisy see Gerbera
Baskets *13*, 35, *116*, 133, *152*; hamper 60, *115*; miniature 115, *116*; see also Trugs, Sussex
Bay see Laurus
Bear's Breeches see Acanthus mollis
Beech see Fagus
Begonia *79*, *86*, 139

Belladonna Lily see Amaryllis
Bellflower see Campanula
Bells of Ireland see Molucella
Berberis 19, 100, *116*, *124*, 139
Bergenia 19, *23*, *51*, 77, *90*, 94, *94*, *125*, *128*, 140
Beta 102
Betula 19, 58, 140
Birch see Betula
Bird of Paradise see Strelitzia
Black-eyed Susan see Rudbeckia
Bladder Senna see Colutea arborescens
Blanket Flower see Gaillardia
Bleeding Heart see Dicentra spectabilis
Bluebell see Scilla
Bocconia see Macleaya
Bottle Brush see Callistemon
Bouquets 129
Box see Buxus
Bracken, to dry 135
Brass containers 37, 133
Brassica 87
Briza gracilis 140
Brodiaea uniflora 140
Brompton Stock see Matthiola
Bronze vases 38
Broom see Cytisus; Butcher's see Ruscus aculeatus; Spanish see Spartium junceum
Buddleia 140
Bulrush see Typha
Bun moss 116, 117
Bunny's Ears see Stachys
Butcher's Broom see Ruscus aculeatus
Buttercup see Ranunculus
Buxus 19, *135*, 140

C

Cactus 86
Caladium 140
Calendula 87, *87*, 140
Calico Bush see Kalmia
Californian Poppy see Eschscholzia
Calla aethiopica see Zantedeschia
Callistemon 59, 140
Callistephus 140
Calluna vulgaris see Erica
Camassia esculenta 51
Camellia 12, 19, 58, 100, 140

Camomile see Anthemis
Campanula 81, 140
Campion see Lychnis
Candidum Lily see Lilium
Candytuft see Iberis
Canna 140
Canterbury Bell see Campanula
Cape Cowslip see Lachenalia
Cape Figwort see Phygelius capensis
Cardinal Flower see Lobelia cardinalis
Cardoon see Cynara scolymus
Carnation see Dianthus
Carpinus betulus 19, 140; to dry 132
Caryopteris clandonensis 140
Cassinia fulvida 140
Catananche 140
Catmint see Nepeta
Ceanothus *126*, 140
Cedrus 19, 100, *126*
Centaurea 59, *114*, 140
Centranthus see Kentranthus
Cephalanthera rubra 14
Cephalaria tatarica see Scabiosa
Chaenomeles *39*, 140
Cheddar Pink see Dianthus
Cheiranthus 24, 60, *61*, *117*, 140
Cherry see Prunus; Cornelian see Cornus mas; Winter see Solanum capsicastrum
Chimonanthus 100, 117, 140, *150*
China Aster see Callistephus
China vases 32, 43, 133
Chincherinchee see Ornithogalum
Chinese Bell Flower see Platycodon grandiflorus
Chinese Lantern see Physalis
Chionodoxa luciliae 140
Choisya ternata 140
Christenings, flowers for 123
Christmas arrangements 123, *126–7*
Christmas Rose see Helleborus
Christmas Tree, decorating a 108
'Chrysal' 22
Chrysanthemum 9, 12, 24, *39*, *45*, *54*, *66*, *86*, 87, *87*, 89, *89*, 100, *100*, *106*, *116*, *121*, *124*, *126*, 128, *128*, *129*, 140
Church arrangements 123–9
Cicerbita alpina 15
Cineraria 19, *36*, 58, 59, *59*, *89*, *102*, 140
Clarkia 140–1

Clematis 9, *38*, 78, *79*, 87, *116*, 141
Clivia 24, 141
Cobaea 87, 90, *90*, 92, 141
Colchicum 87, 88, *88*, *92*, 141
Coleus 141
Colour in arrangements 52–3
Columbine see Aquilegia
Colutea arborescens 141
Cone Flower see Rudbeckia
Cones, flower 47
Containers, flower *30*; brass 37, 133; for children's arrangements 114, 116–17; copper 37, 94, 133; for dried flowers 133; glass 30–1, 43, 70, 133; lead 38; pewter 36, *72*, 74, 133; silver 36, 43, 102, 133; wooden 36, 102, 133; see also Vases, Baskets
Convallaria majalis 25, *30*, 59, *66*, 141
Convolvulus see Ipomoea
Copper containers 37, 94, 133
Coral Bells see Heuchera
Cordyline purpurea *79*, *83*
Coreopsis 141
Cornelian Cherry see Cornus mas
Cornflower see Centaurea
Cornus *106*, *126*, 141; C. mas 19, 100
Cortaderia argentea 141
Corylopsis pauciflora 19, 141
Corylus 19, *67*, 100, 141
Cosmos bipinnatus 141
Cotoneaster 100, *103*, *124*, 141
Cotton Thistle see Onopordon
Crab, Flowering see Malus
Crambe 89
Crataegus 100, 102, 141
Crinum *23*, 87, 141
Crocosmia 141
Crocus 100, 117, 141
Crown Imperial see Fritillaria
Cucurbita 141
Cup and Saucer Plant see Cobaea
Cupid's Dart see Catananche
Cupid vases 32, 33, *135*
Cupressus 103
Currant, Flowering see Ribes
Cut flowers, care of 22–3
Cyclamen 58, 141, *150*
Cymbidium 59, *150*
Cynara scolymus 19, 60, *61*, 62, *62*, 74, 81, *81*, *102*, 141
Cyperus 141

Cypripedium calceolus 15
Cytisus 19, 59, 141

D

Daffodil *see Narcissus*
Dahlia 9, 23, 25, 53, 86, 87, 87, 88, 88, 92, 92, 94, 94, 124, 141
Daisy, Michaelmas *see Aster*
Daphne 14, 58, *59*, 141
Datura 59, 142
Day Lily *see Hemerocallis*
Dead Nettle *see Lamium*
Delphinium 25, 38, 70, 87, *129, 132*, 142
Deutzia 142
Dianthus 12, 14, 38, 45, 59, 65, 72, 72, 76, 81, 102, 114, 121, 126, 129, 142; *D. barbatus 81*, 142
Diapensia lapponica 14
Dicentra spectabilis 142
Digitalis 50, 74, 81, 142
Dimorphotheca 142
Dipsacus sylvestris 142
Dodecatheon 142
Dogwood *see Cornus*
Dome, glass 44
Doronicum 59, 142
Dried flowers 132–5
Driftwood 107
Dyed flowers 12

E

Easter arrangements 123, *124, 125*
Echeveria 58, *79*, 142
Echinops 70, 142
Edelweiss *see Leontopodium*
Elaeagnus 19, *79*, 100, *126*, 142
Elephant's Ears *see Bergenia*
Embothrium 142
Enkianthus campanulatus 142
Epimedium grandiflorum 142
Epipogium aphyllum 15
Eranthis 100, 117, 142
Eremurus 142
Erica 61, 65, 66, 100, 117, *132*, 142
Erigeron speciosus 142
Eryngium 70, 142

Erythronium 38, 58
Escallonia 9, 19, *50*, 74, *74*, 142
Eucalyptus 19, *33, 38, 54*, 72, *72*, 87, *87, 89, 92, 121, 126, 129, 132, 133*, 142; to dry 132
Eucomis 45, 87, 142
Eucryphia glutinosa 142–3
Euonymus 9, 19, *55, 59, 65, 72, 72, 79*, 87, *90*, 100, *102*, 143
Euphorbia 19, 25, *25*, 26, *58, 59, 60, 61, 62, 62, 65*, 67, *67, 83, 124, 128*, 143
Evening Primrose *see Oenothera*
Everlasting Flowers *see Helichrysum, Limonium*

F

Fagus 19, *45, 102*, 143; to dry 132
False Goat's Beard *see Astilbe*
Fatsia japonica 126
Fennel *see Foeniculum vulgare*
Fern, Killarney *see Trichomanes speciosum*; Maidenhair *see Adiantum*; Royal *see Osmunda regalis*
Ferns, to dry 135
Fibreglass vases 39
Firethorn *see Pyracantha*
Flamingo Flower *see Anthurium*
Flax *see Linum*
Fleabane *see Erigeron speciosus*
'Florapak' 46
Flowering Crab *see Malus*
Flowering Currant *see Ribes*
Flowers: blue 53; buying 12; cutting 18, 22; dried 132–5; dyed 12; green 52; orange 53; red 53; wild 13–15; yellow 52–3; *see also* Arrangements, flower
Foam, plastic 46
Foeniculum vulgare 19, 143
Foliage 19
Font decoration 123, *123*
Forget-me-not *see Myosotis*
Forsythia *59*, 100, 117, *117, 124*, 143
Fothergilla major 143
Foxglove *see Digitalis*

Foxtail Lily *see Eremurus*
Freesia 12, *33, 59*, 87, 88, *88*, *115*, 117, *121*, 143
French Marigold *see Tagetes*
Fritillaria 33, 58, 59, *59, 66*, 117, 143
Fuchsia 9, 143
Funkia see Hosta

G

Gaillardia 143
Galanthus 100, 117, 143
Galega 143
Galtonia 25, 143
Garden: miniature 116–17; planning a 16
Gardener's Garters *see Phalaris*
Gardenia 143
Garden Montbretia *see Crocosmia*
Garrya elliptica 100, 143
Gaultheria 143
Gazania splendens 143
Genista 143
Gentiana 15, 36, 59, 87, 89, 117, 143
Geranium *see Pelargonium*
Gerbera 83, 143
Geum 143
Giant Saxifrage *see Bergenia*
Gladiolus 12, *14, 23, 53*, 79, *86*, 87, *97, 121, 124, 128*, 143
Glass containers 30–1, 43, 70, 133
Glass dome 44
Globe Flower *see Trollius*
Globe Thistle *see Echinops*
Gloriosa 82, *83*, 143
Glory of the Sun *see Leucocoryne*
Glycerine 132
Goat's Beard, False *see Astilbe*
Goat's Rue *see Galega*
Godetia 143
Golden Rod *see Solidago*
Gorse, Spanish *see Genista*
Gourds *see Cucurbita*
Gramineae 94
Grape Hyacinth *see Muscari*
Grapes 60, 82
Graphaleum 36
Grass, Black Water 94, *133*
Grasses, Ornamental 135
Guelder Rose *see Viburnum*

Guernsey Lily *see Nerine*
Gum Tree *see Eucalyptus*
Gypsophila 114, 143–4

H

Halesia carolina 144
Hamamelis 100, 144, *150*
Harvest Festival, flowers for 123, *124*
Hawthorn *see Crataegus*
Hazel *see Corylus*
Heath *see Erica*; Blue *see Phyllodoce caerulea*; Common *see Calluna*
Heather *see Erica*
Hebe *see Veronica*
Hedera 9, 19, *32, 38, 61, 65, 66*, 78, *79*, 88, *88, 90, 92*, 94, *94, 97*, 100, *100, 103*, 117, 123, *124, 126*, 144, *150*
Helenium 144
Helianthus 23, *39*, 86, 87, *90, 97, 124*, 144
Helichrysum 106, *133*, 144; to dry 134
Heliotrope, Winter *see Petasites*
Helipterum see Acroclinium
Helleborine, Red *see Cephalanthera rubra*
Helleborus 9, *16, 25*, 26, *33, 38*, 59, *61*, 65, *72*, 100, 117, *129*, 144
Hemerocallis 144
Heuchera 79, 144
Hippophae 144
Holly *see Ilex*; Sea *see Eryngium*
Hollyhock *see Althaea rosea*
Honesty *see Lunaria*
Honeysuckle *see Lonicera*
Hops *see Humulus*
Hornbeam *see Carpinus betulus*
Hosta 19, *39*, 50, 58, *79, 103, 121, 128, 129*, 144
Houseleek *see Sempervivum*
Hoya carnosa 32
Humulus 86, 87, 123, 144
Hyacinth *see Hyacinthus*; Grape *see Muscari*; Summer *see Galtonia*; Wild *see Scilla*
Hyacinthus 9, *33, 38, 54*, 58, *59, 59*, 100, 117, *117*, 123, 144; *H. candicans see Galtonia*
Hydrangea 23, 26, 27, *38*, 59, 87, 88, *88, 124*, 128, 144; to dry 134
Hypericum 115, 144

I

Iberis 144
Iceland Poppy *see Papaver*
Ilex 19, 100, *103*, 123, *126*, 144
Immortelle 106
Indian Shot Plant *see Canna*
Ipomoea 144
Iris 12, *38*, 58, 60, *61, 79, 93*, 100, 117, *144*
Ivy *see Hedera*
Ixia 61, 144

J

Japonica *see Chaenomeles*
Jasmine, Common *see Jasminum*; Madagascar *see Stephanotis*
Jasminum 100, *100*, 117, 144–5
Jerusalem Cowslip *see Pulmonaria*
Jerusalem Sage *see Phlomis*
Juniperus 145

K

Kaffir Lily *see Schizostylis*
Kalenchoe 79, 145
Kalmia 145
Kentranthus 53, 145
Kerria japonica 145
Killarney Fern *see Trichomanes speciosum*
Kniphofia 86, *94, 94, 97*, 145

L

Lachenalia 59, 145
Lady's Mantle *see Alchemilla*

155

Lady's Slipper *see Cypripedium calceolus*
Lamb's Ears *see Stachys*
Lamb's Tongue *see Stachys*
Lamium 19, *61*, 145
Larch *see Larix*
Larix 19, 58, 106, 145
Larkspur *see Delphinium*
Lathyrus 27, 58, 70, *70*, 72, *72*, 78, *79*, *88*, *114*, 145
Laurel, Common *see Prunus*; Spotted *see Aucuba*; to dry 133
Laurus 16, *126*, 145
Laurustinus 117
Lavandula 145
Lavatera 145
Lavender *see Lavandula*; Cotton *see Santolina*; Sea *see Limonium*
Load containers 38
Leontopodium 145
Leopard's Bane *see Doronicum*
Leucocoryne 145
Leucojum 145
Leycesteria formosa 145
Liatris 145
Lichen 106
Ligustrum 9, 19, 87, *87*, *100*, 145
Lilac *see Syringa*
Lilium 32, 70, *79*, 81, *83*, *97*, *121*, *124*, 145
Lily *see Lilium*; African *see Agapanthus*; Arum *see Zantedeschia*; Belladonna *see Amaryllis*; Candidum *see Lilium*; Day *see Hemerocallis*; Foxtail *see Eremurus*; Guernsey *see Nerine*; Kaffir *see Schizostylis*; Madonna *see Lilium*; Peruvian *see Alstroemeria*; Scarborough *see Vallota*; Snake's Head *see Fritillaria*; Snowdon *see Lloydia serotina*; Torch *see Gloriosa*; True *see Lilium*; Water *see Nymphaea*
Lily-of-the-Valley *see Convallaria majalis*
Lily-of-the-Valley Tree *see Pieris floribunda*
Lime *see Tilia*
Limonium 145; to dry 134
Linaria 145
Linum 145
Liriope 9
Lloydia serotina 14
Lobelia cardinalis 145
Lonicera 19, *51*, *79*, *90*, 145
Lords and Ladies *see Zantedeschia*
Love-in-the-Mist *see Nigella*
Love-Lies-Bleeding *see Amaranthus caudatus*
Lunaria 79, 145; to dry 134

Lupin *see Lupinus*
Lupinus 25, *74*, 81, *81*, 145
Lychnis 138, 145–6

M

Macleaya 19, 146
Madagascar Jasmine *see Stephanotis*
Madonna Lily *see Lilium*
Magnolia 58, 106, *133*, 146
Mahonia 19, 100, *100*, *103*, *126*, *129*, 146
Maidenhair Fern *see Adiantum*
Maidenhair Fern Tree, plastic 110
Malcolmia maritima 146
Mallow *see Lavatera*
Malus 55, 77, 146
Maple *see Acer*
Marble vases 31, 78
Marigold, African *see Tagetes*; French *see Tagetes*; Pot *see Calendula*
Matthiola 59, *74*, 87, 146
May *see Crataegus*
Maypole *114*
'Mazie' *47*
Meadow Rue *see Thalictrum dipterocarpum*
Megasea see Bergenia
Mexican Orange Blossom *see Choisya ternata*
Mezereon *see Daphne*
Michaelmas Daisy *see Aster*
Mignonette *see Reseda*
Milk Thistle *see Silybum*
Mimosa *see Acacia*
Miniature gardens 116–17
Minuartia stricta 15
Mistletoe *see Viscum album*
Mock Orange *see Philadelphus*
Molucella 90, 146; to dry 134
Monarda didyma 146
Monkshood *see Aconitum*
Montbretia *see Tritonia*; Garden *see Crocosmia*
Morning Glory *see Ipomoea*
Moss 45; bun 116, 117, 'Mosy' *46*
Mother-in-law's Tongue *see Sansevieria*
Mountain Ash *see Sorbus aucuparia*
Mouse Plant *see Arisarum*

Mullein *see Verbascum*
Muscari 33, *55*, 58, *59*, *66*, *79*, 117, *117*, 123, 146
Myosotis 33, 59, 114, 117, *117*, 146
Myrtus 100

N

Narcissus 12, *33*, *38*, 58, 59, *59*, 66, *67*, 100, *117*, *124*, 146
Nasturtium *see Tropaeolum majus*
Nemesia strumosa 146
Nepeta 81, 146
Nephrolepsis 103
Nerine 87, 94, *94*, 102, *102*, 146
Netting, Wire 42–3, 133
Nettle *see Coleus*; Dead *see Lamium*
New Zealand Daisy Bush *see Olearia haastii*
New Zealand Flax *see Phormium*
Nicotiana 38, *39*, 70, *86*, *87*, 146
Nigella 81, 146
Nymphaea 146

O

Oak, to dry 132
'Oasis' *46*, 133
Obedient Plant *see Physostegia virginiana*
Oenothera biennis 146
Olearia haastii 146
Onion *see Allium*
Onopordon 19, 146
Opium Poppy *see Papaver*
Orach *see Atriplex*
Orchid, Ghost *see Epipogium aphyllum*; Military *see Orchis*; Monkey *see Orchis*; Poor Man's *see Schizanthus*
Orchis 15
Ornithogalum 146, *150*
Osmanthus 19, *33*, 58, *65*, *86*, *86*, *94*, *94*, *103*, 146–7
Osmunda regalis 147

P

Paeonia 19, *47*, *51*, 81, *81*, *90*, 122, *124*, 128, 147
Paeony *see Paeonia*
Pampas Grass *see Cortaderia argentea*
Pansy *see Viola*
Papaver 12, *55*, 147
Parsley, Wild *12*
Partridge in a Pear Tree 108
Pasque Flower *see Pulsatilla vulgaris*
Passiflora caerulea 9, *65*, 147
Passion Flower *see Passiflora caerulea*
Peach *see Prunus*
Pelargonium 9, 19, *32*, *53*, *61*, *65*, *66*, *77*, *79*, 147
Pennisetum 88, 102
Penstemon 147
Periwinkle *see Vinca*
Pernettya mucronata 147
Peruvian Lily *see Alstroemeria*
Petasites 117, 147
Petunia 147
Pewter containers 36, 72, 74, 133
Phalaris 19, *38*, *39*, 147
Pharbitis *see Ipomoea*
Philadelphus 59, 147
Phlomis 81, *103*, 147
Phlox 70, 87, 147
Phormium 19, *121*, 147
Phygelius capensis 147
Phyllodoce caerulea 15
Physalis 133, 147; to dry 134
Physostegia virginiana 147
Phytolacca 23, 87, 147
Picture, flower, *132*
Pieris floribunda 19, 100, 147; *P. japonica 66*, 147
Pine *see Pinus*
Pineapple 82
Pineapple Flower *see Eucomis*
Pinholders 44, 133
Pinks *see Dianthus*
Pinus 9, 106, 123, 147
Pittosporum tenuiflorum 147
Plastic foam 46
Plastic vases 39
Platycodon grandiflorus 147
Plum *see Prunus*
Plumbago 150
Poinsettia *see Euphorbia*
Polyanthus 103, 123
Polygonatum 19, *38*, *51*, 59, *83*, *88*, *90*, 147
Polygonum baldschuanicum 147; *P. bistorta 51*
Poor Man's Orchid *see Schizanthus*
Poppy *see Papaver*;

Californian *see Eschscholzia*; Iceland *see Papaver*; Shirley *see Papaver*
Potentilla 102, 147
Primrose 116, 123; Evening *see Oenothera biennis*
Primula 55, 58, 59, *59*, 117, *117*, 147–8, *150*
Privet *see Ligustrum*
Pruning 16
Prunus 19, 24, *53*, 58, 62, *62*, *92*, 100, 117, 148; *P. lusitanica 121*, *125*
Pulmonaria 19, *66*, 117, 148
Pulsatilla vulgaris 33, *79*, 139, 148
Pussy Willow *see Salix*
Pyracantha 19, 100, *126*, 148
Pyrethrum 148

Q

Quaking Grass *see Briza gracilis*
Quince *see Chaenomeles*

R

Ranunculus 33, 59, *59*, 117, 148
Red Hot Poker *see Kniphofia*
Red Ink Plant *see Phytolacca*
Reed Mace *see Typha*
Reseda 87, 148
Rhamnus cathartica 100
Rheum palmatum 148
Rhododendron 12, 19, 58, *61*, 74, 77, *77*, *83*, 148; to dry 133; *see also Azalia*
Rhubarb *see Rheum palmatum*
Rhus cotinus 53, *106*, 148; *R. typhina* 148
Ribbon Grass *see Phalaris*
Ribes 19, 58, 148
Robin on a Standard Holly Tree 111
Rodgersia pinnata 148
Romneya 148
Rosa 12, 26, *26*, 27, *33*, 70, 87, 148; *R. alba maxima* 70, *121*; *R.* 'Baccara' *102*; *R.* 'Belle de Crécy'

70; R. 'Blanc Double de Coubert' 76, *76*; R. 'Brownie' 94, *94*; R. *canina* 100, 102; R. 'Cardinal Richelieu' 27, *70*; R. 'Carol' 72, *92*, *102*; R. 'Cecile Brunner' *30*, *89*, 114; R. 'Charles de Mills' *70*; R. *chinensis viridis* 79; R. 'Constance Spry' 16, *70*, 72, *72*; R. 'Dream Girl' 88, *88*; R. 'Evergold' *121*; R. *gallica* 102; R. 'Garnet' *102*, R. 'Golden Rain' *31*, 79; R. 'Golden Showers' 97, *97*; R. 'Iceberg' *82*, *121*; R. 'Jenny Wren' *70*; R. 'La Follette' 16, *76*, 76; R. 'La Minuet' *81*; R. 'Madame Ernst Calvat' *70*; R. 'Madame Isaac Pereire' *70*; R. 'Madame Pierre Oger' 27; R. 'Magenta' *74*; R. 'Mercedes' *102*; R. 'New Dawn' *50*; R. 'Paul's Scarlet' *31*, *82*; R. 'Peace' *124*; R. 'Pitica' *79*; R. 'Rosemary Rose' *76*; R. *rubrifolia* 53; R. 'Spanish Sun' *65*; R. 'Vesper' 94, *94*; R. 'Virgo' *50*
Rose *see Rosa*; Christmas *see Helleborus*; Guelder *see Viburnum*
Rosemary *see Rosmarinus*
Rosmarinus 19, *100*, *126*, 148
Rowan *see Sorbus aucuparia*
Royal Fern *see Osmunda regalis*
Rubus 92
Rudbeckia 86, *86*, 87, 97, 148
Rue *see Ruta*; Goat's *see Galega*; Meadow *see Thalictrum dipterocarpum*
Ruscus aculeatus 148
Russian Vine *see Polygonum baldschuanicum*
Ruta 16, 19, 65, *103*, *114*, *123*, 148

S

Sage *see Salvia*
St John's Wort *see Hypericum*
Salix 19, *67*, 100, 117, *117*, *124*, *126*, 148
Salpiglossis 94, *94*, 148
Salvia 19, *70*, *89*, 148
Sambucus 88, 92
Sand 45

Sansevieria 148
Santolina 19,148
Saxifraga cernua 14; S. *cespitosa* 15
Saxifrage, Drooping *see Saxifraga cernua*; Giant *see Bergenia*; Tufted *see Saxifraga cespitosa*
Scabiosa 38, 53, 70, 88, *88*, 148
Scabious *see Scabiosa*
Scarborough Lily *see Vallota speciosa*
Schizanthus 148
Schizostylis 148
Scilla 24, 33, 54, 59, 60, 61, 67, *67*, 117, 148
Scots Broom *see Cytisus*
Sea Buckthorn *see Hippophae*
Sea Holly *see Eryngium*
Seakale 89
Sea Lavender *see Limonium*
Sedum 9, *79*, 88, 90, *124*, 148-9
Sempervivum 149
Senecio 19, 61, *102*, *103*, *126*, 149; S. *cineraria see Cineraria*
Shells, as containers 65, 115, *116*
Shirley Poppy *see Papaver*
Sidalcea 149
Silver containers 36, 43, 102, 133
Silybum 149
Smilacina 19, *83*, 149
Smilex *see Asparagus*
Smoke Tree *see Rhus cotinus*
Snake's Head Lily *see Fritillaria*
Snapdragon *see Antirrhinum*
Snowball Tree *see Viburnum*
Snowberry *see Symphoricarpos*
Snowdon Lily *see Lloydia serotina*
Snowdrop *see Galanthus*
Snowdrop Tree *see Halesia carolina*
Soapstone vases 31
Solanum capsicastrum 149
Soldiers and Sailors *see Pulmonaria*
Solidago 39, 70, *86*, 97, 149
Solomon's Seal *see Polygonatum*
Sorbus aria 19, 59, 62, *62*, 74, *128*, 149; S. *aucuparia* 149
Southernwood *see Artemisia*
Sow-Thistle, Alpine *see Cicerbita alpina*
Spanish Broom *see Spartium junceum*
Spanish Gorse *see Genista*

Spartium junceum 149
Spiked Speedwell *see Veronica spicata*
Spindle Tree *see Euonymus*
Spiraea 19, 149
Spring flowers 58-67
Stachys lanata 19, 60, *61*, 149
Stag's Horn Sumach *see Rhus typhina*
Star of Bethlehem *see Ornithogalum*
Statice *see Limonium*
Statice sinuata *97*, *132*; to dry 134-5
Stems, flower: which bleed 25-7; hard 22, 24; hollow 25; smelly 27; soft 22, 24-5; needing special treatment 27
Stephanotis 149
Stock, Brompton *see Matthiola*; Virginia *see Malcolmia maritima*
Stones, decorative 47
Strawberry, Wild 32
Strawberry Tree *see Arbutus*
Straw Flower *see Helichrysum*
Strelitzia 149, *150*
'Styrofoam' 47, 133
Summer flowers 70-83
Summer Snowflake *see Leucojum*
Sunflower *see Helianthus*
Sweet Peas *see Lathyrus*
Sweet Sultan *see Centaurea*
Sweet William *see Dianthus barbatus*
Symphoricarpos 19, 76, *86*, 88, *88*, *90*, 100, 149
Syringa 24, *24*, *51*, 59, 74, 77, 100, 149

T

Table Centre with Mistletoe 111
Table decorations 55, 59, 66; miniature garden as 117
Tagetes 149
Taxus 100, 149
Teazle *see Dipsacus sylvestris*
Teesdale Sandwort *see Minuartia stricta*
Tellima 51, *90*, 129
Thalictrum dipterocarpum 149
Thistle, Globe *see Echinops*
Thistle, Milk *see Silybum*

Thorn Apple *see Datura*
Thrift *see Armeria*
Tilia 81, *81*, 106, *121*, 149; to dry 132
Toadflax *see Linaria*
Tobacco Plant *see Nicotiana*
Torch Lily *see Gloriosa*
Tradescantia 66, *103*, 149
Tricholaena rosea 94
Trichomanes speciosum 15
Tritonia 149
Trollius 59, 149
Tropaeolum majus 149
Trug, Sussex 22, 35
Tsuga canadensis 100
Tubes, flower 47
Tulip *see Tulipa*
Tulipa 12, 24, 25, 59, *61*, 77, 100, 117, *124*, 149
Tussilago farfara 117
Typha 19, *128*, 149

U

Umbrella Plant *see Cyperus*
Urn-shaped vases 55, 89

V

Valerian *see Kentranthus*
Vallota speciosa 149
Vases 30-3; alabaster 31, 72, 78; bronze 38; china 32, 43, 133; cupid *32*, 33, *135*; fibreglass 39; glass 30-1, 43, 70, 133; imitation marble 31; improvised 39; marble 31, 78; plastic 39; soapstone 31; urn-shaped 55, 89; wall 38; *see also* baskets,
Veratum nigrum 70, 87
Verbascum 19, 150
Verbena 87, 150
Veronica 16, 38, 65, *103*, 150; V. *spicata* 14
Viburnum 19, 24, 58, 59, 66, *67*, 72, 100, *100*, 117, 150
Vinca 150
Vine *see Vitis*; Russian *see Polygonum baldschuanicum*
Viola 27, *114*, 116, 117, 150
Violet *see Viola*
Virginia Stock *see Malcolmia maritima*
Viscum album 100, *123*, 150
Vitis 19, 87, 150

W

Wallflower *see Cheiranthus*
Wall vases 38
Wandering Jew *see Tradescantia*
Water Lily *see Nymphaea*
Waterlily with Tinsel Candle 110
Watsonia 150
Wayfaring Tree *see Viburnum*
Wedding arrangements 128-9
Whitebeam *see Sorbus aria*
Willow *see Salix*
Winter Aconite *see Eranthis*
Winter Cherry *see Solanum capsicastrum*
Winter flowers 100-7
Winter Heliotrope *see Petasites*
Winter Jasmine *see Jasminum*
Wintersweet *see Chimonanthus*
Wire netting 42-3
Wisteria 150
Witch Hazel *see Hamamelis*
Wooden containers 36, 102, 133; *see also* Trug, Sussex
Woodsia alpina 14; W. *ilvensis* 14
Wormwood *see Artemisia*

Y

Yarrow *see Achillea*
Yew *see Taxus*
Yucca 150

Z

Zantedeschia 24, 65, *125*, 150
Zinnia 38, 53, 87, 94, *94*, *116*, *124*, 150

Photographs by
Malcolm Robertson